Reprints of Economic Classics

IRISH ECONOMICS
1700 - 1783

[HENRY R. WAGNER]

IRISH ECONOMICS

1700-1783

A BIBLIOGRAPHY WITH NOTES

[1907]

REPRINTS OF ECONOMIC CLASSICS

AUGUSTUS M. KELLEY · PUBLISHERS

NEW YORK 1969

First Edition 1907

(London: *Privately Printed*, J. Davy & Sons, The Dryden Press, *8 & 9 Frith Street, Soho W*, 1907)

Reprinted 1969 by

AUGUSTUS M. KELLEY · PUBLISHERS

New York   New York   10001

·   ·   ·   ·   ·   ·   ·   ·   ·   ·   ·

S B N   678 00559 1

L C N   79 95162

·   ·   ·   ·   ·   ·   ·   ·   ·   ·   ·

PRINTED IN THE UNITED STATES OF AMERICA
by SENTRY PRESS, NEW YORK, N. Y. 10019

IRISH ECONOMICS:

1700-1783

A BIBLIOGRAPHY WITH NOTES

[Privately Printed]

LONDON

J. DAVY & SONS

THE DRYDEN PRESS 8 & 9 FRITH STREET SOHO W.

1907

INTRODUCTION.

I examined most of these works while engaged in studying the development of Banking in Ireland during the eighteenth century, and extracted a large number of notes from such as had any bearing on that subject. Finding myself obliged to leave London, before I had time to incorporate the substance of these notes in a monograph, and it being unlikely that I should have an opportunity during the next few years to complete the work, I decided to print simply the Titles with the notes attached, in the hope that they would prove of some' use to other students of Irish Economic History.

As the time at my disposal was very short, I have been obliged to omit entirely, or reduce to very small proportions, the notes which I had taken from the better known works. Time was also lacking to re-write the notes, and, therefore, in many cases they appear as originally jotted down.

The Libraries were examined in the following order :—
    The British Museum.
    Trinity College, Dublin.
    The Halliday Collection to 1735.
    The Bradshaw Collection in the Library of the University of Cambridge.
    The Halliday Collection from 1735 on.

Most of the tracts to which the Press-Mark of the British Museum is attached, are also to be found in the Halliday Collection.

After having examined these libraries, I fortunately discovered a few tracts, which I had not seen previously, in the possession of E. R. McClintock Dix, Esq., the Irish Bibliographer, who very kindly gave me permission to examine them.

I beg to tender my thanks to the officials of Trinity College Library, Dublin, The Royal Irish Academy, and the Library of the University of Cambridge, for the assistance which they have very kindly given me in making these researches.

HENRY R. WAGNER.

January, 1907.

ABBREVIATIONS.

B.M.—British Museum.

H.C.—Halliday Collection, Royal Irish Academy, Dublin.
> When followed by a number, the number of the volume in the bound part of the Collection is indicated.
> When no number is given, the copy is to be found in the Boxes in which the unbound pamphlets are arranged according to date.

T.C.D.—Trinity College, Dublin.

U.C.—University of Cambridge, Bradshaw Collection.

D.N.B.—Dictionary of National Biography.

D.P.E.—Dictionary of Political Economy.

b. t.—besides title.

b. f. t.—besides false title.

b. t. & f. t.—besides title and false title.

IRISH ECONOMICS: A BIBLIOGRAPHY,
1700-1783.

1. SEASONABLE PROPOSALS For a perpetual FUND OR BANK IN
DUBLIN. For the Improvement both of LANDS and TRAFFICK,
suitable to the *Trade, Money*, and *Business* of IRELAND, both in
Relation to *England* and other Foreign Parts: Maturely Calculated, both for the present Juncture, and the General Good of
the said City and Kingdom, and Particular Advantage of all the
Subscribers; who now, if they please may securely make
above 20 *per Cent. per Ann.* clear Profit of their Money.
The intended Methods are Drawn and Improved, both from
a true Experience, and by the best Examples of all the *Banks*
in *Europe*: It is therefore humbly proposed by *Richard Holt*,
of *London*, Merchant, and others, to proceed as followeth, *viz.*

I. THAT at *Dick's* Coffee House in *Skinner Row*, near the *Exchange* in *Dublin*; a
Book pursuant to the following Proposals, shall be speedily prepared and
lye open daily, from Nine till Twelve, and from Three till Six of the Clock, for the
space of one Month, or until One Hundred Thousand Pounds, or more, be Subscribed
by any Persons whatsoever, who please to subscribe themselves, or order the Subscrib-
ing thereof by others; at which Place these printed Proposals may be had Gratis; also
Attendance shall be there given, to Answer Objections which will be made by a few
Goldsmiths and Scriveners, and perhaps by some Merchants who deal by Exchange,
and have not yet duly consider'd these Matters.

II. That no Person shall Subscribe less than 50 l. nor above 5000 l. in this Fund,
until the last Six Days of the limited time; and each Person having 100 l. Interest
therein in his own proper Right, shall have one Vote in all Elections, and other
Matters hereafter to be Debated; and no Person whatsoever shall have more than
one Vote.

III. That no Person shall be capable of being a Trustee, or Director in this Bank,
who hath not 500 l. Interest, or more on his own Name, and in his own proper Right,
during all the time he shall so Act.

IV. That within Six Days after the said Fund shall be compleated to the Satisfac-
tion of the Subscribers, of which at least Three Days Publick Notice shall be given,
and fixed upon the Exchange; there shall be a General Meeting of the Subscribers
Qualified to Vote; who by Ballating, shall choose from amongst themselves a Committee of Fifteen such Persons, as by the Majority of Votes shall be Esteemed fittest
to be Trustees, or Directors for the Trust and Management of the said Fund, until
the first Day of *May* 1697, or until others shall be Elected and Invested into the said
Trust, by the said General Assembly; which Election shall always hereafter be in the
Month of *April* every Year.

V. That within Three Days after the said Election shall be made and declared, the
said Directors shall Meet and Elect out of themselves, a Chairman; and always afterwards at every General Meeting of the said Directors, a Chairman out of the Majority

of them shall be Elected, and always by Ballating all Elections shall be made whatsoever.

VI. That the Trustees and Directors for the time being, or the Majority of them together, shall by the Majority of Votes, have Power to Decide all Questionable Matters relating to the said Bank, or Compa, and every, or any part thereof, and full Power of the whole Management of the Joynt-Stock ; to Buy, or Purchase, or Lend on Securities, for the said Compa ; and to prepare Rules, Orders and Methods, and to choose all other Officers and Servants, and to pay them their respective Salleries : But all, or any of the said Officers, Servants Rules, or Orders, shall, or may be Approved, Confirmed, Altered, or Rejected by a General Assembly of the Proprietors, which at any time the Directors (or if they refuse then any Five of the Proprietors Qualified to Vote) shall have Power to call together : and the said General Assembly shall Limit, and Appoint what Salleries the several Directors shall have ; and shall have Power also, if to them it shall seem meet at any such General Meeting to displace any of the said Directors, or Trustees, and to choose others in their Rooms.

VII. That all Persons whatsoever, who shall be concerned in this Joynt-Stock or Fund, shall be True and Faithful to the Joynt Interest thereof, and shall Acquiess in, and perform all Determinations, Rules, and ·Orders of the Majority of the said Proprietors, under the Penalty and Forfeiture of such part of His, Her, or Their Interest in this Fund, as the said Directors for the time being shall think meet ; all which Forfeitures and Penalties, shall be to the Use and Benefit of this Bank.

VIII. That the Subscribers shall Transfer to the said Trustees and Directors their respective Interests, in Trust for the said Proprietors, in such manner, and to such fit and proper Uses, as the Nature and Improvement of this Bank doth require ; which Trust, the said Trustees and Directors are also to except ; for which purpose, a Draught of a Deed of Settlement in due time shall be prepared for their Approbations ; by which all needful Provisions shall be made, and especially these two which next follow, *Viz.*

IX. That the said Directors and Trustees in their own particular Persons and Estates, shall be effectually Secured and Indemnified for their Acting ; except for willful Fraud, or Breach of Trust ; in which Cases, the Person Guilty only shall be Chargeable.

X. The said Directors and Trustees, or the said Subscribers, or Owners of the said Fund, in their Persons or Estates, shall not be liable for more, or further than their own respective Proportions in the said Fund, nor shall at all be concerned one for another.

XI. That within one Month next after the Election of the said Trustees and Directors, the said Subscribers shall pay in unto them the said Trustees, or unto whomsoever they shall Direct or Appoint, ten pounds *per Cent.* of all their said Respective Subscriptions, and 15 l. *per Cent.* more, within Four Months next after the said Election, except the said Second Payment be longer deferr'd by the General Assembly ; and the other remaining Three Quarter Parts shall be paid afterwards at Three or more Payments successively, and all within Twelve Months after the said Election, at such set times, and in such manner as the said Directors for the time being, shall appoint and call in the same.

XII. That if any of the said Subscribers shall fail, or make default of Payment of His, Her, or Their first Payment of 10 l. *per Cent.* within the said time of one Month, as is hereby limited ; it shall be lawful for any other Person or Persons approved by the said Directors, immediately after the Expiration of the said one Month, to pay in the same, and to receive and take the Benefit of His, Her, or their Subscriptions ; but if within the time limited there be not above 50000 l. Subscribed, then the said Subscriptions shall be void, or not obliging to any Subscriber.

XIII. That there shall be always made two Dividends of the Profits of the said Bank every Year ; but that nothing except the clear Profits, or Revenue of this Fund shall ever be Divided ; so that the whole Original Joynt Stock as it shall be now Subscribed, and hereafter Invested, or Secured, shall always remain Full and Intire, or be by the same Proprietors augmented and improved to such further and greater Fund, as shall from time to time by them be thought fittest, for the Joynt-Interest of the said Bank, Accommodation of Trade, and Security to all Persons who shall give Credit to the same.

XIV. That if all the Monies paid in by the Subscribers, shall (*Communibus annis*) produce above 10 l. *per Cent. per ann.* clear Profit ; the above Named *Richard Holt,* for his Pains in the Composure of these Proposals, and for his Advice, Time, and Charges, in and about the same, shall have and enjoy, to him and his Heirs, *&c.* one Shilling out of every 20 Shillings of clear Profits, which shall be Gained by, or Arise from this Fund, or any part thereof, to any Person or Persons whatsoever; and also the benefit of the Transfers, so long as the said Fund, or Bank shall continue to produce the Profit as aforesaid; and that all Dividends and Ballances of Accounts, as they shall stand Stated in the Bank Books, shall always be Conclusive, and without any further Account to be given, either in Law or Equity.

XV. That whatsoever herein shall be found short Expressed or Imperfect, may from time to time be added unto, Explained or Amended, pursuant to the true Interest and Meaning thereof, by a General Assembly of the Trustees, Directors, and Owners of the said Fund, or as by Learned Council shall be reasonably advised, or devised; and that humble Application may in due time be made to the High Court of Parliament, to encourage and establish this Undertaking, in such manner as in Their Great Wisdom, shall thereupon be thought most fit.

XVI. That to prevent Delays, and to incourage the first Beginners to Subscribe; the first Subscriber shall have 5 *per Cent.* the second 4 and half *per Cent.* the third 4 *per Cent.* allow'd and repaid him; and so on to the 10th Subscriber, who also shall have half *per Cent.* repaid him, and all out of the first Payment only, but no further.

"*It may seem a Paradox, that this* Bank *should lend Money Cheaper, and yet* "*Gain above* 20 per Cent. per Ann. *But whosoever enquires into all the Three* "*Banks lately set up in* London, *will find, they lend Money at* 3, 4, *and* 5 per "*Cent. and yet every Subscriber in any of the said Three Banks, has already* "*Gained; or may have, when he pleases, above* 50 per Cent. *clear Profit for all* "*his Money Paid in.*

2 folio sheets.

T.C.D.—33. *q.* 22 (16).

Besides the account of the Petition presented to the House of Commons and printed in the proceedings of that session, nothing more seems to be known about this project. It was referred to a Committee of the House, which apparently never made any report. The idea is evidently taken from that of the Bank of Scotland, and it is quite likely that some of the promoters of the Bank of Scotland were interested in this scheme as well.

The Richard Holt referred to in this Proposal is probably the same Holt that was interested in the Patent for Tin Farthings in England some years previously.

1705]

2. An Essay Towards the Improving of the Hempen and Flaxen Manufactures In The Kingdom Of Ireland. By Louis Crommelin Overseer of the Royal Linnen Manufacture of that Kingdom.

4to. Dublin: Printed by Andrew Crook Printer to the Queen's most Excellent Majesty, on the Blind Key. 1705.

Tit. 4 pp. Dedication to Duke of Ormonde. 43 pp. Text + 5 pp. Description of Plates + 7 Plates.

Reprinted in sm. 4to in 1734 by R. Owen on 43 pp. and as other edition.

3. Some Thoughts Humbly offer'd Towards an Union Between Great-Britain And Ireland.

London: Printed for John Morphew near Stationers-Hall 1708.

Title. 2 Pref. 29 pp. 4to.

One of the earliest Tracts on the Subject and written in what for the Times was a very liberal spirit.

The Author deprecates the jealousy of Ireland which existed in England, and asserts "that prohibitions of all kinds are not only unnatural but very destructive to Trade."

(3)

4. Observations On Raising the Value Of Money. Wherein the
Interest of Ireland is particularly Consider'd. In a Letter
to a Friend. ......
   *Dublin: Printed by Samuel Fairbrother, and are to be
   Sold at his Shop in Skinner-Row, over-against the Tholsel,
   1718. Price Two-Pence.*
      Sm. 8vo. 16 pp.
      B.M. 8227, *aa.* 13.
   Letter dated *Wicklow, May* 8, 1718, says the City of Dublin is
   much alarmed by a Report that the Gold Coins were to be reduced in
   proportion to Silver in order to keep the Silver in the Kingdom, and
   that a Proclamation would be issued to enforce the Weighing of Gold
   Coin as formerly.
   Quotes Petty and Temple against raising money, and adopts Locke's
   arguments about equal quantities of silver = always equal quantities
   of silver. Assumes silver as the measure of value. Says "Credit is
   the expectation of money within some limited time." Dislikes to see
   the silver go, because the scarcity will give rise to the necessity of
   half-pence, and speaks of the prodigious currency of light and deceitful
   money. Well-written tract.

5. A Proposal For the universal Use Of Irish Manufacture, In
Cloaths and Furniture of Houses, etc. Uterly Rejecting and
Renouncing Every Thing wearable that comes from England.
   *Dublin: Printed and Sold by E. Waters, in Essex-street
   at the Corner of Sycamore-Alley,* 1720.
      8vo. 15 pp.
      By Jonathan Swift.
      T.C.D.—R.R. pp. 57, *no.* 9.
   This Tract which was written in the latter part of 1720, makes
   mention at the end of a project for a Bank. The author intimates
   that he is going to attack the project of which he says he understands
   one half the money will be real and the other half only Gasconnade.
   The Tract made a great sensation, and brought about a vigorous and
   persistent prosecution of Waters, the printer. It is, I believe, the
   earliest Tract of Swift's relating to the Economic affairs of Ireland
   and is reprinted in all collections of his Works. Swift frequently
   refers to this Tract in his correspondence. It was answered by the
   following and also by "A Defence of English Commodities, being an
   Answer to the Proposal for the universal use of Irish Manufactures:
   with an Elegy upon the Death of Mr. De Mar, the famous rich man,
   who died at Dublin, July 6, 1720," published in 8vo, Dublin, 1720.
   This Tract is also attributed to Swift by Lowndes, but without any
   good reason, although the Elegy may be by him.
   Re-issued in 1734 in sm. 8vo, from some Collection with a new title
   page.

6. An Answer To The Proposal For The Universal Use Of Irish
Manufactures, And utterly rejecting and renouncing every
Thing that is wearable that comes from England. ...,........
   Dublin: Printed 1720.
      Sm. 8vo. 16 pp.
      H.C. 51.

(4)

7. The Swearer's-Bank: Or, Parliamentary Security For Establishing a new Bank In Ireland. Wherein The Medicinal Use of Oaths is considered. (With The Best in Christendom. A Tale.) Written by Dean Swift. .... To which is prefixed, An Essay upon English Bubbles. By Thomas Hope, Esq;

Dublin: Printed by Thomas Hume, next Door to the Walsh's-Head in Smock-Alley. 1720. Reprinted at London by J. Roberts in Warwick-Lane.

Half Title. Title. viii. 15.

8vo.

By Jonathan Swift.

Some doubt has been thrown on the authorship of the Essay on English Bubbles. It was accepted by Faulkner and is now generally ascribed to Swift. I have never seen the separate original Imprint nor the original Dublin Edition of "The Swearer's Bank." I think it is quite possible, that the Essay on Bubbles may have never been published separately but only as an introduction to "The Swearer's Bank."

The commonest Editions of this Tract are the 3rd, printed by Thomas Hume, Dublin, 1721, and Curll's Reprint, London, 1721, in 23 pp. 8vo.

8. The Sin of With-holding Tribute, By Running of Goods, Concealing Excise, etc. Laid open and Addressed to the Trading Part of the Nation. By Jasper Brett, M.A. Chancellor of the Cathedral of Connor. ....

Dublin: Printed by Samuel Fairbrother, and are to be Sold at his Shop in Skinner-Row, over against the Tholsel, 1721

8vo. 39 pp.

T.C.D.—Gall. L. 3. 45. no. 4.

9. The Present Miserable State of Ireland. In a Letter From a Gentleman in Dublin to his Friend in London.

(at end) *London Printed: And Re-printed in Dublin by Sarah Harding in Molesworth's Court in Fishamble-Street,* 1721

1 folio sheet (signed J. S. Dublin, Sept. 1721).

I discovered the original of this Tract in a Letter printed in Mist's "Weekly Journal," September 30, 1721. The Letter is introduced by a few remarks to the effect, that it was written "by an eminent Dublin Trader in the Woolen Affair, to a rich Gentleman of distinction settled in London," and is signed "S. T.," and dated "Dublin, March 15, 1720-21."

The Time of this reprint is doubtful, although printed as 1721. Sarah Harding was certainly not printing regularly until after the death of John Harding in the early part of 1725, and the General appearance of this Broadside would indicate that it was printed 1726-7. The initials signed to the Letter have been changed from "S. T." to "J. S.," with the evident object of ascribing it to Jonathan Swift; and the date has been changed from the original date to the date of printing in Mist's Journal.

The Tract was discovered by Sir Walter Scott, evidently reprinted in 12mo. It appears in the appendix to Vol. I of Scott's Works, and was also reprinted in Temple Scott's edition of Swift, and was without date or publisher. Scott probably ascribed it to Swift on account of this signature, which he considered to be a good evidence. But the reasons which he gives turn out to be entirely mistaken ones, inasmuch as the Tract was really written in 1721, and, indeed, his reasoning on the subject was very far-fetched, as the Letter has extremely little resemblance to Swift's Letter to the Earl of Peterborough.

It is not impossible, however, that this Tract was really written by Swift, as it contains many of the ideas which Swift was continually bringing before the Public from 1720 on. In a Tract published in 1740, there is a reference to it as having been printed about 3 years before, which was probably the date of the appearance of the 12mo reprint, which Sir Walter Scott saw.

10. Reasons Offer'd for Erecting a Bank in Ireland; In A Letter To Hercules Rowley, Esq. By Henry Maxwell, Esq.
    Dublin: Printed by Aaron Rhames, and are to be Sold by the Booksellers. 1721.
    63 pp.
    B.M. 8227, *aaa.* 29.

Apparently reprinted 1755.

This Tract of Maxwell's, besides containing the Case for the Bank, is devoted to a discussion of the Economic effects of reducing the rate of interest, and devotes some attention to the industrial state of Ireland, and the land question. Maxwell contends that the price of commodities is entirely independent of rent, and governed by the market only, and that the price of land does not govern the price of its unmanufactured products, but that the reverse is the fact.

The attempt to organize this Bank failed, probably owing to the discredit into which—at the moment—all Corporations had fallen. There is not much information about it, except what is contained in the following Pamphlets and the proceedings of the Irish Parliament. A Summary of the arguments for and against the Bank, as published by Maxwell and Rowley, is given by Monck Mason. Lawson, in his History of Banking, gives an account of the affair, with very full extracts from proceedings in Parliament.

11. An Answer To A Book, Intitl'd, Reasons offer'd for erecting a Bank in Ireland. In A Letter To Henry Maxwell, Esq; By Hercules Rowley, Esq;
    Dublin: Printed by and for Geo. Grierson, at the two Bibles, in Essex-Street. MDCCXXI.
    8vo. 51 pp.

Letter dated Nov. 23, 1720, but seems to be a mistake, as Maxwell's Letter was printed in 1721, to which this is an answer.

Another Edition. Same title, but:—
    Corke: Re-Printed by and for George Bennett, and are to be sold at his Shop opposite broad Lane.
    8vo. 26 pp.
    B.M. 8227, *aaa.* 33.

Rowley strives to raise all the prejudices possible, but some of his objections are well taken. The strongest objection was that the money would probably all be loaned on real security.

A great jealousy of monied corporations still existed, as is curiously shown by his assertion, that "in England merchants seldom borrowed from the Bank, but usually from the Goldsmiths."

12. His Grace Charles Duke of Grafton, Lord Lieutenant General and General Governour of Ireland, His Speech to both Houses of Parliament, at Dublin, on Tuesday the 12th Day of September, 1721. Published by Authority.

(at end) *Dublin: Printed by Andrew Crooke, Printer to the King's Most Excellent Majesty, at the King's-Arms in Copper-Alley, 1721.*

1 folio sheet.

T.C.D.—33.q. 22 (15).

Announcing that the King has directed that a Commission be passed under the Great Seal of Ireland for receiving voluntary Subscriptions in order to Establish a Bank. The King leaves matter to Parliament in what manner it may be settled.

13. Mr. Maxwell's Second Letter To Mr. Rowley; Wherein the Objections Against the Bank are Answer'd.

Dublin: Printed by Aaron Rhames, and Sold by the Booksellers. 1721.

8vo. 29 pp.

B.M. 8227, *aaa.* 30.

14. An Answer to Mr. Maxwell's Second Letter to Mr. Rowley, Concerning the Bank. By Hercules Rowley, Esq ;

Dublin: Printed by and for Geo. Grierson, at the two Bibles, in Essex-Street. MDCCXXI.

8vo. 24 pp.

B.M. 8223, *a.* 41.

15. Remarks on Mr. Maxwell's and Mr. Rowley's Letters : Setting forth the Advantages of a Bank and Lumbards in Ireland. In a Letter to a Friend.

Dublin: Printed by Aaron Rhames, and are to be Sold by the Booksellers. 1721.

8vo. 30 pp. + 1 Err. at end.

B.M. 8227. *Aaa.* 28.

Seems from this that ordinary Inland Bills were drawn seldom less 10-12 days sight, and that the charge was 3d. or 4d. in the pound up to 6d. for 28 days sight.

16. A Letter To The Gentlemen Of The Landed Interest In Ireland, Relating To a Bank............

Dublin: Printed by and for Aaron Rhames, and sold by the Booksellers. 1721.

8vo. 32 pp.

B.M. 8227. *aaa.* 19.

Says that the chief business of the town is now carried on by paper issued by Tradesmen.

This is a very able, well-written tract, and possibly written by a private Banker or money-lender in Dublin. Refutes Rowley's arguments (being an answer to Rowley's Answer to Maxwell). Insinuates that the movement was brought on by the Treasury Dept., which, owing to lack of specie, was obliged to receive private bills in payment of customs.

17. A Letter To A Member of Parliament Touching the Late Intended Bank............
   Dublin: Printed, and are to be Sold by the Booksellers, MDCCXXI.
   8vo. 23 pp.
   T.C.D.—R.R. kk. 26, *no.* 12.
   Generally attributed to F. Hutchinson.

   Thinks £500,000 all the specie Ireland can have use for, and that so far never more than £400,000 has been in circulation. If more was in circulation, it would leave the country to go to some other country, where it might be employed to greater advantage. Therefore thinks the proposal to issue paper money will have this effect. Chief reasons for objecting seemed to be the unsettled condition and danger of invasion. Also danger of a large and powerful corporation.

   On the 29th of September the Commons did Resolve in favour of the Bank. Says the fund to secure the Public must be sufficient, valuable, permanent and accessible. The Bonds proposed to be given only bind the Party during his Life, and the security is, therefore, not permanent.

18. Strange Collection of May-Be's Fully Answered and Cleared Up. By a Subscriber and Well-Wisher to the Bank:
   (*Dublin:* 1721).
   1 folio sheet, printed on both sides.
   T.C.D.—Press A, 7, 6, *no.* 3.

   Issued in favour of the Bank in answer to criticism which appeared at large in a " Letter touching the intended Bank."

   Says this Bank was first set on foot in Ireland in May, 1720, by a Person of no fortune or interest in Ireland, and during the South Sea Excitement.

   Says the uncharitable, inquisitive and censorius Disposition of Ireland has already lost Sir A——r C——s's Million Bank and the Insurance Office, and now threatens to lose this Bank.

19. Objections against the general Bank in Ireland as it Stands now Circumstanciated, whether it Do's or Do's not Receive a Parliamentary Sanction, in Answer to a Letter from a Gentleman in the City to his Friend in the Country.
   (at end) *Dublin: Printed by G. C.* 1721.
   Two 4to leaves, signed Patriophilus Misolestes.
   Dix.

   Fears either the temptation will prove too great for servants of the Bank, in spite of the Regulations, or the English Government will wish to borrow the Cash, in which case the chief men in the Bank—being also in Posts under the Government—will not be able to refuse. If private Bankers fail, only a few are hurt, but the fate of the whole Kingdom will lie in the hands of this Bank.

   If Paper be made current coin, and interest reduced, the Bank would become possessed of mortgages on most of the Estates in Ireland, most of which are now more or less encumbered, and thus secure all the power which naturally would attend such a position.

20. A Letter to Henry Maxwell, Esq ; Plainly shewing the Great Danger that the Kingdom has escaped, and the great

Inconveniences, that must of Necessity have happen'd, if a Bank had been establish'd in this Kingdom............

Dublin: Printed by Thomas Hume in Smoak-Ally, 1721.

8vo. 19 pp.

T.C.D.—33. *q.* 22 (13).

Thinks the expense of management would be great. The Bankers and money-lenders will fight it, and mentions the clergy as money-lenders at 8 per cent.

Speaks of large numbers of merchants, who are nothing but Factors at 2½ per cent. commission for foreign, especially Dutch merchants. The clergy will fight the Bank, and in Postscript says there is a sheet hawked around already, which he intimates is by Swift (A List of Sub-scribers).

Really in favour of the Bank, and written during the controversy and not after, as indicated on the Title-page.

21. A Dialogue Between Mr. Freeport, a Merchant, and Tom Handy, a Trades-man, Concerning the Bank.

(at end) *Printed in the Year* MDCCXXI.

Broadside.

T.C.D.—33. *q.* 22. (18).

Custom was for 15 days' bills Inland exchange, and apparently Exchange was 3d. 4d. and 6d. per Pound for these Bills which made, allowing for transit, 18 to 21 days in running.

According to this the Proposed Bank was to lend money on non-perishable goods at 5 per cent. for not exceeding 3 months.

Favours highly the Bank.

22. Whereas nothing can be a greater Security, that the BANK of IRELAND with the Powers granted to it, Shall be Well and Faithfully Managed, as well with the Regard to the Sub-scribers as to Those who shall either Trust or Transact with the Same, than that a good and prudent Choice be made of a Governor, Deputy Governor, and Twelve Directors. To the Intent that every Person who has Subscribed Five Hundred Pounds, or upwards, for His or Her proper Use, and not in Trust for another, may have Time maturely to Consider in whose Hands they Judge proper to place so great a Trust. The Commissioners appointed to receive Subscriptions for Erecting a Bank have order'd the following List to be Printed, with Marks distinguishing those who are Qualified to be chosen Governor, another Mark distinguishing those who are Qualified to be chosen Deputy Governor or Directors, and another Mark distinguishing those who are only Qualified to give their Votes in the several Elections. Every Person qualified to Vote, is hereby desired to Write a List of the Persons Names which He or She shall Judge proper to be chosen Governor, Deputy Governor and twelve Directors, and that they may Write the word Governor, Deputy Gov-ernor and Director, after each of the Names in their List respectively in a Scrole of Paper Roled up, to the Intent that, according to the Majority of Votes, the several Officers may be Chosen.

Mark for a Person Qualified to be chosen Governor——————————— ***
Mark for Person Qualified to be chosen Deputy Governor or Director ——— **
Mark for a Person Qualified to Vote ———————— *

A.

*** The Right Honourable Earl of Abercorn.
** Mr. John Aigoin, Merchant.
* John Allcock, Esq;
* Mr. John Anderson
* Colonel John Archer
* Mr. John Armstrong.

B.

** Right Honourable Lord Viscount Boyne.
*** Colonel Thomas Bligh
** Brinsly Butler, Esq;
** Mrs. Elizabeth Bligh, Widow
* Mrs. Katherine Bligh
* Mrs. Hannah Bligh
** Colonel Thomas Bellew
** Mr. Francis Bonham
* Mr. Peter Bere Merchant
* Mr. Edward Butler
** Thomas Burdit, Esq;
* Mrs. Ann Bureau, Widow
*** Captain Edward Brice
* Mr. William Binauld
* Francis Burton, Esq;
* Francis Bernard, Esq;
* Mr. William Barry
* Mr. James Brown, Merchant
* Mr. William Bourke
* Samuel Bindan, Esq;
* Robert Brown, Esq;
* Mr. Lewis Bertin, Merchant
* Mr. Henry Burrows, Merchant.

C.

** The Honour. Thomas Coote, Esq;
** Charles Coote, Esq;
*** Mr. Robert Clements, Junior.
*** John Coddington, Esq;
** Brigadier James Crofts
* Captain Gabriel Canafilhs
* Colonel Joseph Campbell
** Mr. Daniel Coningham, Merchant.
** David Chaigneau, Esq;
* Mr. Nicholas Cassel
* Michael Cuffe, Esq;
* Mr. Lewis Cromelin.
* Mr. William Clarke, Merchant.
* Mr. Elias Crips
* William Crosby, Esq;
* Christopher Chamberlin, Esq;
* Mr. Stephen Costilloe
* Thomas Crosby, Esq;
* Theophilus Clements, Esq;

D.

** Rt. Rev. Lord Bishop of Dromore
* Rt. Rev. Lord Bishop of Downe
*** Joshua Dawson, Esq;
** Arthur Dobbs, Esq;
* The Reverend Archdeacon Daniel

* Captain William Duponset
* Capt. Theophilus Debrizay, Sen.
* Capt. Theophilus Debrizay, Jun.
* Mr. John Darquier
* Mr. Walter Davey, Merchant
* John Dawson, Esq;
* Mrs. Ann Dowling
* Mrs. Katherine Downs
* Colonel Daniel Debernatre
* Major Charles Decreferont

E.

** Charles Echlin, Esq;
** Edward Eyre, Esq;
** Eyre Evans, Esq;
* The Reverend Robert Ecklin
* Mr. James Ecklin
* Mr. William Empson, Merchant
* Captain Isaac Estaunie
* Mr. Caleb Emerson
* Thomas Evans, Esq;
* Benjamin Everard, Esq;

F.

** The Right Honour. Lord Ferrard
*** James Forth, Esq;
** Michael Fleming, Esq;
** Mr. Daniel Falkiner, Banker
* Sir William Fowns, Kt.
* Mr. John Finlay, Merchant.

G.

*** Luke Gardiner, Esq;
*** Mr. Holland Goddard, Merchant in Cork.
** Mr. John Goddard, Merchant in London
* Mr. Nicholas Grueber, Merchant
* Mr. Thomas Green
* Mr. Godfrey Green
* Mr. Thomas Gibson, Merchant
* Mr. Lewis Griffith
* Edward Griffith, Esq;
* Captain Henry Gresmes
* Alexander Graydon, Esq;
* James Grattan, M. D.
* Mr. Thomas Gleadowe, Merchant
* Mr. John Galbaly, Merchant
* Mr. Isaac Gervereau

H.

* Rowley Hill, Esq;
* Mr. John Hall
* The Hon. Henry Hamilton, Esq;
* The Hon. Capt. Gustavus Hamilton
* Mr. John Healy
* Mr. James Howison
* Mr. Charles Howison, Merchant
* Hannibal Hall, Surgeon.
* Mr. William Hamilton
* Mrs. Ann Hall
* Mr. James Hamilton
** Rolston Humphrys, Esq;

I.

** John Irwin, Esq;
** Richard Jackson, Esq;
* Thomas Jackson, Esq;
* Mr. William Jackson
* Lewis Jones, Esq;
* Mr. William Jones

K.

* John Kennedy, Esq;
** Edmond Knapp, Esq; Alderman of Cork.

L.

*** The Right Honourable the Lord Viscount Limerick
** Nicholas Licet, Esq; Limerick
* Captain Mathew Lafitt
* Mr. Ralph Leland
* Mr. James La Rimbliere

M.

* The Honourable Justin Macarty, Esq;
*** Thomas Medlicot, Esq; one of the Commissioners of His Majesty's Revenue.
*** Henry Maxwell, Esq;
*** Thomas Marley, Esq;
*** James Macartney, Esq;
** Isaac Manley, Esq;
** John Manly, Esq;
** Mr. William Montgomery, Mer.
* George Macartney, Esq;
** Mr. Richard Maguire, Banker.
* The Reverend Peter Maturin
* Patrick Mitchell, M. D.
* Mr. Stephen Mazyke, Merchant
* Mr. William Moore, Merchant
* Lady Margaret Maxwell
* James Manson, Esq;
* George Martin, M. D.
* Mr. Robert Mills
* The Reverend John Maxwell
* Mr. William Maple
* William Maynard, Esq;
* Robert Macusland, Esq;
* Mr. James Maculla.
* Philip Morel, Esq;
* Captain Malcom Macneal
* William Montgomery, Esq;

N.

*** Brigadier Robert Napier.
** Mr. Joseph Nuttal, Banker.
* Captain Toby Norris,
* Mr. William Noy.
* Mr. Alexander Nesbit.

O.

* Mr. Henry O Hara

P.

*** The Right Honourable Benjamin Parry, Esq;
*** John Pratt, Esq;
** Alderman John Porter
** John Preston, Esq;

* Henry Purdon, Esq;
* Mr. Lambert Pepper,
* Nathaniel Preston, Esq;

R.

** Henry Rose, Esq;
*** Philip Rawson, Esq;
** Mr. John Rieuset, Merchant
* Major David Renovard
* Mr. William Ryves, Merchant

S.

*** The Right Honourable Oliver St. George, Esq;
* Henry Sandford, Esq;
*** James Stevenson, Esq;
*** Mr. James Swift, Banker
*** Richard Sherlock, Esq;
* Francis Edmond Stafford, Esq;
** Mr. John Shaw, Merchant
* Mr. Silvanus Shore, Merchant
* Fielding Shaw, Esq;
* Mr. Simon Sandys
* William Stephens, M. D.
* The Reverend Archibald Stewart
* Ezekiel Stewart, Esq;
* William Stewart, Esq;
* Reverend James Smith
* Mrs. Ann Smith Widdow.
* Mr. Patrick Smith Merchant Belfast.

T.

*** Sir Thomas Taylor, Bart.
*** Thomas Taylor, Esq;
* Robert Taylor, Esq;
* Reverend Archdeacon Rob. Taylor
* Mr. John Taylor.
* James Topham, Esq;
* Mr. William Tighe
* Capt. John Charles Terote

V.

** Agmondisham Vesey, Esq;
** William Vesey, Esq;
** Barron Daniel Virazell
** George Vaughan, Esq;
* Thomas Upton, Esq;
* Mr. John Verrailles, Merchant
* Mr. Anthony Verrailles, Merchant
* Alderman John Vincent, Limerick
* Christopher Usher, Esq;

W.

*** Michael Ward, Esq;
** Major General Owen Winne, Esq;
* Captain Owen Wynne.
* Hugh Willoughby, Esq;
** Robert Waller, Esq;
* John Walker, Esq;
* John Walsh, Esq;
* Mr. William Westland
* Mr. Hugh White, Merchant
* Nicholas Ward, Esq;
* Edward Webber, Esq;

Y.

* The Reverend Dean John Yeard.

23. Subscribers to the Bank Plac'd according to Their Order and Quality. With Notes and Queries.
    (begins) A True and Exact Account, etc.
    (at end) *Dublin : Printed by John Harding in Molesworth's Court in Fishamble Street.*
    1 sheet folio.
    By Jonathan Swift.
    B.M. 1890. *e.* 5. (161).

    Very amusing skit on the proposed Bank. Ridicules the subscribers on account of some being French and others mostly low traders, or women. From this it seems that only 7 of the nobility, 1 Baronet and 1 Knight, 6 Clergymen, and 41 Members of the House of Commons were subscribers.
    This is reprinted as an addition to "The Eyes of Ireland Open," in Roberts' Reprint of the latter Tract in London, 1722.

24. A Letter from a Lady in Town to her Friend in the Country, concerning the Bank Or, The List of the Subscribers farther Explain'd.
    (at end) *Dublin : Printed by John Harding.*
    Broadside printed on both sides. Dated, Dublin, Dec. 1, 1721.
    By Jonathan Swift.
    Dix.

    Reprinted in "The Eyes of Ireland Open."

25. A Letter To The K—— at Arms. From a Reputed Esquire, One of The Subscribers to the Bank.
    [Dated Nov. 18, 1721].
    (at end) *Dublin : Printed by John Harding in Molesworth's-Court.*
    Broadside.
    By Jonathan Swift.
    T.C.D.—Press. A. 7. 6. *no.* 4.

    Evidently a take-off on some prominent Subscriber. No information of economic interest.

26. A MS. List of Officers of Bank of Ireland chosen *Nov.* 20, 1721
    H.C.

E. F. Abercorn, Gov.
Sr Tho. Taylor, Sub.-Gov.

Directors.
Oliver St. George
Michael Ward
Henry Rose
Henry Maxwell
Tho. Coote
James Macartney
Joshua Dawson
John Pratt
Brinsley Butler
Agmondisham Vesey
James Stephenson

Nov. 24 the Governor and Directors apply'd to the Lord Lieutenant for an Incorporated Charter. His Grace desired time to consider.

On Nov. 8th, already the House of Lords had agreed that a Bank would be prejudicial and of extreme ill consequence to this Kingdom.

27. An Account Of The Short Life, sudden Death And Pompous
Funeral, Of Michy Windybank, Only Child to Sir Oliver
Windybank.
Printed in the Year 1721.
8vo. 8 pp.
Dix.

Insinuates that Sir Oliver was an insolvent debtor.
Only a skit. Probably refers to Oliver St. George.

28. The Last Speech and dying Words Of The Bank of Ireland.
Which was Executed at College-Green, on Saturday the 9th
Inst.
(at end) *Dublin: Printed by John Harding in Moles-
worth's-Court in Fishamble-Street.* (*n.d.* but 1721).
Broadside printed on one side.
Dix.

Not by Swift, as regrets the loss of the Bank, and says he believes
"we have less Sense and more evil Nature in this Kingdom than in
any other Part of Europe ; I believe more, Ireland will never get anything
for its Advantagè, we not having Judgment to know whether it be so,
or not, and more, its the Opinion under Hand of all our Writers, that
we ought never to have a good Thing, or any Credit, because it may
be applied to an evil Use, a Way of arguing, that wou'd destrpy every
good Thing in being."

29. The Bank's Ghost Appearing to the People of Ireland, Or, An
Answer to the Last Speech and Dying Words of the Bank.
(at end) *Dublin Printed*, 1721.
Broadside printed on one side.
Dix.

A skit, badly written and printed.

30. Resolutions of the House of Lords in relation to the intended
Bank in this Kingdom.
(at end) *Dublin: Printed by Andrew Crooke, Printer to
the King's most Excellent Majesty, at the King's-Arms in
Copper-Alley*, 1721.
Broadside printed on one side.
Dix.

Prints the Resolutions of Nov. 8th and Dec. 16th, and the order
of the House of Dec. 20th to print them.
Resolution of the 8th Nov. : "That the Erecting this Bank may
prove Prejudicial and of extreme ill Consequences to this Kingdom."
Resolution of Dec. 16th : "That if any Lord shall Sollicit or
Attempt the Erecting of a Bank, or Procuring a Charter, or aiding or
abetting, without the Consent of Parliament, He shall be Judged to
Obstruct His Majesties Service, and shall be Deemed a Contemner of
the Authority of this House, and a Betrayer of the Liberty of his
Country."

31. The Phoenix, Or, A New Scheme For Establishing Credit, Upon the most solid and satisfactory Foundation, and intirely free from all Objections made to the former intended Bank. By John Irwin, Esq; ....

Dublin : Printed by Thomas Hume, next Door to the Walsh's Head in Smock-Alley, 1721

8vo.   14 pp.

T.C.D.—33. *q.* 22. 5.

Irwin says he had proposed a Bank the year before, which did not meet the approval of the Legislature.   Therefore he proposes this, a Parliamentary Bank of £500,000, based on a redeemable fund of £25,000 yearly, settled on some branch of the Revenue ; £500,000 notes to be issued, payable on demand.   If the Bank has no money, it may assign securities, or may issue a Sealed note at 5 per cent. interest, at option of the party, chargeable on the said fund of £25,000.   All notes to be accepted in Revenue payments.   Deposits to bear interest at the rate of 1d. per day of £100 or thereabouts. Notes to be lent at 5 per cent. on land or 6 per cent. on goods, bills, &c.

32. A Letter To the Reverend Dr. Swift Dean of St. Patrick's Dublin ; Relating to the present State of the Manufactures of Ireland.

12mo.   8 pp.   Signed Roger Kendrick.

(at end) *Dublin, Printed by C. Carter,* 1721.

H. C. 51.

From a Member of the Weavers, giving an account of their grievances.

33. The Bank thrown down.   To an Excellent New Tune.

(at end) *Dublin.   Printed by John Harding in Molesworth's Court.*

Broadside.

B.M. 839. *m.* 23 (93).

Another Edition, Reprinted in Mountrath-street, 1721.

Most amusing poetical skit on paper money.   Written in Swift's style, and probably by him.

34. The Eyes of Ireland Open.   Being, A Short View of the Project for Establishing The Intended Bank of Ireland : With some Remarks upon its Managers, Promoters and Progress. In a Letter from a Lady at Dublin to her Friend in the Country.   To which is added, A Description of the Subscription, Or, A true and exact Account of the Nobility, Gentry and Traders, Who Are Subscribers to the Bank, Extracted from the List Published by Order of the Commissioner appointed to receive Subscriptions, And Interspers'd with Notes and Queries.   The Second Edition.

London : Printed from the 2nd Edition of the Dublin Copies, for J. Roberts in Warwick-Lane, 1722.

8vo.   28 pp.

B.M. 8225. *a.* 26.

(pp. 19-28 incl. are a Reprint of the folio sheet of the Pamphlet

commencing " Subscribers to the Bank Plac'd according to their Order
and Quality," and ascribed to Swift).
The Letter is dated Dublin, Dec. 1, 1721.
A Reprint of No. 23 and 24, with some additional matter inserted.

35. Some Considerations For The Promoting of Agriculture And
Employing The Poor.
Dublin : George Grierson, MDCCXXIII.
8vo. 44 pp.
T.C.D.—P.OO. 50. *no.* 11.

An extremely interesting Tract, advocating various reforms of
which Craik gives a resumé in his "Life of Swift," 2nd edition,
pp. 144, 5.
The Preface is signed R.L.V.M., that is, Lord Molesworth.

36. Considerations Upon Considerations For the Promoting of
Agriculture, And Providing for the Poor.
Dublin : G. Ewin. (d. Nov. 10, 1723).
Title, 4 Dedication. 72 pp.
T.C.D.—P. oo. 50.

2nd Edition, 1724, with Additions and Alterations.
H.C. 60.

37. A Letter To A Member of Parliament Concerning the Imploy-
ing and Providing For The Poor.
Dublin : Aaron Rhames, 1723.
8vo. 16 pp.
T.C.D.—P. oo. 50. *no.* 9.

38. Ireland's Consternation In the loosing of Two Hundred Thousand Pound of their Gold and Silver for Brass Money. Set
forth by an Artificer in Metals, And a Citizen of Dublin.
Shewing the fatal Consequences of Coining in another Kingdom Three Hundred Tun Weight of Copper Half-pence,
amounting to the Damage of Two Hundred Thousand Pounds
Sterl. to the Nation, and the Continuance of the same for
Fourteen Years.
n.d. n.p. (but before August 23rd, 1723.)
4 pp. folio. By James Maculla.
T.C.D.—Press A. 7. 2. (*no.* 41.)

Says the coins are made out of Irish copper, sent to Bristol and not
refined. A smelting company are the real undertakers, and they have
ingrossed all the mines and ores in Ireland to be sent to England for
smelting and refining.
This is very early, as a note at end says a large quantity has now
been landed and part already got into circulation, some accepting and
some declining, part lighter than the rest and badly made, so as to
invite counterfeiting. In a Tract printed 1728 Maculla claims that he
was the first person to discover the ill consequences that Wood's Coins
might have in Ireland.

NOTE AS TO WILLIAM WOOD.

William Wood, according to Philip Nelson's "Coinage of Ireland," was born in 1671 and resided at the Deanery, Wolverhampton, from 1692 to 1713, and died in London 1730.

Besides this Copper Coinage for Ireland, he also executed a Copper Coinage for the American Colonies, which experienced a somewhat similar fate to the Irish Coinage.

Wood was extensively engaged in Mining and Smelting operations, and it is highly probable that these Coinage schemes were entered into as an adjunct to that business. From a notice published in Mist's Weekly Journal of June 18, 1720, it seems that Wood had secured a lease on the property of the Governor and Societies of the Mines Royal and Mineral and Battery Works in certain counties—in all, in fact, except Devonshire and Cornwall. No doubt among these properties were the Smelting Works of Neath Abbey, belonging to the Mines Royal Company, and this, therefore, explains the statement made by Grant Francis in his "Smelting of Copper in the Swansea District," that "the copper used by Wood for the Coinage was made in the Neath Abbey Works."

Copper had been discovered in Cornwall about 30 years before to be in marketable quantities; but in the early stage of the business the ore was considered of no value, and was bought in Cornwall as low as £2 10s. per ton for 7 to 10 per cent. ore. The business was largely in the hands of the Quakers of Bristol, and before 1720 there were certainly Works near Bristol.

The large profits made out of this business were probably the inducement which brought Wood into it, as in a Broadside, entitled "The Present State of Mr. Wood's Partnership," published about 1720, Wood proposes "to give better prices for ores than hitherto and also sell the metal cheaper," and states that "they have already bought ores in Cornwall."

The latest and best information regarding Wood's coins and the manufacture of them, is contained in Philip Nelson's "Coinage of Ireland," 1905, but the matter is referred to at length in almost all the late editions of Swift's Works, and the affair is dealt with in great detail both in Coxe's "Memoirs of Sir Robert Walpole" and Monck Mason's "The History and Antiquities of St. Patrick."

39. The True State of the Case Between the Kingdom of Ireland of the one Part, and Mr. William Wood of the other Part. By a Protestant of Ireland.

(at end) *Dublin : Printed by John Harding in Molesworth's-Court.*

8vo. 8 pp. no regular title.

T.C.D.—R.R. pp. 57. (*no.* 9.)

Written evidently in 1723. Already Wood's coins are not all the same, and some that were brought in are claimed to be counterfeits.

There is plenty of half-pence of the old Patent in the country, and they only need a few farthings. Very calm and yet forceful protest against the Half-pence. Ascribed in T.C.D. Cat. to Swift.

This Tract is reprinted in the Appendix to Vol. I. of Sir Walter Scott's Edition of Swift from the above copy in Trinity College, Dublin. Temple Scott, however, omits it in his recent Edition of Swift's Works.

It is probable that this is the Tract, generally ascribed to the Earl of Abercorn, which Swift mentions in his Letter to Lord Carteret of April 28th, 1724.

40. The Pattentee's Computation of Ireland, In a Letter from the Author of the Whitehall Evening-Post concerning the making of Copper-Coin. As Also the Case and Address Of Both Houses of Parliament, Together with His Majesty's most Gracious Answer, To The House of Lord's Address.

Dublin : Printed by John Whalley in Arundel-Court just without St. Nicholas Gate 1723.

4to. 12 pp.

H.C.

The Contents consist of :

A Letter signed A.B. in favour of Wood.

An Answer to same, signed C.D.

Ireland's Case, Humbly presented to the Honourable the Knights, Citizens and Burgesses in Parliament assembled.

The Addresses of both Houses of Parliament in 1723 to the King.

The Answer by the King.

The Tract must, therefore, have appeared in the latter part of 1723, or possibly in January or February of 1724.

In the Letter containing Wood's Defence it was asserted that copper, ready for coinage at the Mint, cost 18d. per lb., the cost of coinage 3½d., and other expenses 2d. per lb. He would have to sell the coin at a discount of 5 per cent. to allow—as he says—for exchange, leaving a profit of only 1½d. per lb. over and above the costs as given above,—which, however, he admits also carried a profit in the manufacture.

This Position is also repeated and insisted on in Walpole's Correspondence, as given by Coxe, and, indeed, it seems highly probable, that considering there was also an import duty in Ireland on the coin, that Wood's profit—after paying £1,000 a year to the Crown and the Comptroller, and reimbursing himself for the original outlay of £10,000—would have been very small, if the terms of the Patent had been strictly complied with. Under the terms of the Patent 60 halfpence were to be coined to the pound, while in the English coinage at the time 1 lb. of copper was struck into only 46 halfpence. But this difference was defended on the ground of the general lower value of Irish currency, and the increased expenses of putting the coins into circulation.

The arguments in favour of Wood's coinage may be reduced to the following propositions :—Ireland wants copper coin ; the Quantity would be no inconvenience ; they are better than any hitherto—or probably ever will be ; the King will lose nothing, the Public will gain, and the Kingdom will have £100,000 additional current cash.

" Ireland's Case " is reprinted in Temple Scott's Edition of Swift. Mr. Scott thinks that the compilation was gotten out in Wood's interest, but I cannot agree to this, as—in my view—the evident intention of the Pamphlet is to discredit Wood.

41. A Letter To The Shop-Keepers, Tradesmen, Farmers, and Common-People of Ireland, Concerning the Brass Half-Pence Coined by M^r. Woods, With a Design to have them Pass in this Kingdom.

Wherein is shewn the Power of the said Patent, the Value of the Half-Pence, and how far every Person may be oblig'd to take the same in Payments, and how to behave in Case such an Attempt shou'd be made by Woods or any other Person.

(Very Proper to be kept in every Family). By M. B. Drapier.

Dublin: Printed by J. Harding in Molesworth's-Court.
Sm. 8vo. 16 pp.
By Jonathan Swift.
B.M., C. 58. *b.* 18. (1.)

There has been considerable controversy about the date of the publication of this Tract. Near the beginning Swift states that "about three years ago a little book was written to advise all people to wear the manufactures of this our own dear country." As that Tract was published with the date of 1720, it would naturally follow that the present Tract was at least written in 1723. When Faulkner reprinted the Tract in 1725 in the "Hibernian Patriot," the word "Three" was changed to Four, thus indicating that the date of this Tract was 1724. Mr. Nelson says that the Tract was published in April 1724, but I do not know what his authority is for this. From a careful reading of it, I should be inclined to place the writing of it at least as somewhat nearer the Addresses of the Houses of Parliament to the King in September, 1723. I have seen it asserted that the Tract was published in November, 1723, but although I know nothing to prove that such is not the fact, it seems probable that Mr. Nelson's date is more nearly correct.

Reprinted in "The Hibernian Patriot" and in all subsequent editions of Swift's works.

42. A Letter To Mr. Harding the Printer, Upon Occasion of a Paragraph In His News-Paper of Aug. 1st. Relating to Mr. Wood's Half-Pence.

By M. B. Drapier. Author of the Letter to the Shop-Keepers, etc.

Dublin: Printed by John Harding in Molesworth's-Court in Fishamble-Street.
16 pp. sm. 8vo. Dated Aug. 4, 1724.
The Second Drapier Letter (by Swift.)

Reprinted in all editions of Swift.

43. Another Letter To Mr. Harding the Printer, Upon Occasion of the Report of the Committee Of The Lords of His Majesty's Most Honourable Privy-Council, In Relation to Mr. Wood's Half Pence and Farthings, &c. lately Publish'd.

1 Folio Sheet, signed "Misoxulos."
B.M. 8145. *h.* 1. (16.)

Mr. Mason considers that this Broadside was probably written by Swift, but it is also attributed to Sheridan.

44. A Letter From A Lady of Quality To Mr. Harding the Printer, Occasionally Writ upon the General Out-Cry Against Wood's Halfpence.

Dublin: Printed by John Harding in Molesworth's-Court in Fishamble-Street, 1724.
8 pp. Signed "Hibernia." Aug. 22, 1724. sm. 8vo.
T.C.D.—R.R. pp. 57.

A Skit, suggesting that the Ladies assemble and move an Address to his Gracious Majesty.

Probably by Swift, and after the 1st and 2nd Drapier Letters.

45. A Word or Two To The People of Ireland, Concerning The Brass Money that is, and shall be Coin'd by Mr. Woods, and which he is endeavouring to Impose upon Us.

By a Well-wisher to his Country.

Dublin: Printed by John Harding in Molesworth's-Court in Fishamble Street.

12mo. 16 pp.

H.C.

Written after 1st and 2nd Drapier's Letters. Generally urging people to refuse to take them, suggests a kind of religious boycott against those who give or take the half-pence.

46. The Report of the Committee Of The Lords of his Majesty's most Honourable Privy-Council, in relation to Mr. Wood's Half-Pence and Farthings, etc.

n. p. n. d.

Folio. 4 pp. (dated July 24th, 1724).

T.C.D.—Press A, 7, 1, no. 122.

Looks like London printing.

47. Some Observations Upon a Paper Call'd The Report Of The Committee Of The Most Honourable the Privy-Council In England, Relating to Wood's Half-Pence. By M. B. Drapier. Author of the Letter to the Shop-Keepers, etc.

Dublin: Printed by John Harding in Molesworth's Court in Fishamble Street.

Sm. 8vo. 32 pp. (dated Aug. 25, 1724).

By Jonathan Swift.

The Third Letter. Contains a *resumé* of the previous patents for coining copper farthings and half-pence, and says he received the above Report, without place or position, but thinks it to have been printed in Dublin, probably the copy being from the London Journal.

A 4th Edition was issued of this corrected.

H.C. 62.

Reprinted in all editions of Swift.

48. A Letter To The Whole People of Ireland. By M. B. Drapier. Author of the Letter to the Shop-Keepers, etc.

Dublin: Printed by John Harding in Molesworth's-Court in Fishamble-Street.

Sm. 8vo. 22 pp. (dated Oct. 13, 1724).

By Jonathan Swift.

The Fourth Letter. Mentions in this a Paper printed in Bristol and reprinted in Dublin.

Also attributes a tract printed in London, favouring Wood to one Coleby, who gave evidence before the Committee of the Privy Council on this matter.

2nd Edition same year, same with sheet of errata added.

H.C. 62.

Reprinted in all editions of Swift.

49. Some Considerations on the Attempts made to pass Mr. Wood's brass money in Ireland. By a lover of his country.
  Dublin.
  Folio. 4 pp.
  By David Bindon.

  This Tract was reprinted in "The Hibernian Patriot." I have not seen the original of this.

50. Some Reasons Shewing the Necessity the People of Ireland are under, for Continuing to refuse Mr. Wood's Coinage. By the Author of the Considerations...... ......
  Dublin : Printed in the Year MDCCXXIV.
  8vo. 28 pp.

  This is one of the best tracts on the subject of Wood's copper money, far superior to Swift's ; indeed, it seems possible that the facts in Swift's third letter were taken from it.
  This was reprinted in the "Hibernian Patriot," 1725 and 1730, and ascribed by Faulkner to Swift, or at least his words may be so construed.
  The ded. however, is signed D.B., and this copy has in MS. on title page : David Bindon Esq.
  Also reprinted in the "Hibernian Patriot."

51. A Defence of The Conduct Of The People of Ireland, In their unanimous Refusal of Mr. Wood's Copper-Money. Wherein all the Arguments advanced in Favour of it, are particularly considered.
  Dublin : Printed for George Ewing, at the Angle and Bible in Dames-Street, MDCCXXIV.
  8vo. 39 pp.
  B.M. 8145, *a.* 27.
  2nd Edition by Ewing in 45 pp., same year.

  This is also an extremely well-written Tract, containing the history of Irish Copper Coinage and an account of the proceedings in relation to Wood's Patent. It contains a copy of the Report of the Assayers, appointed by the Privy Council, to investigate the charges made against Wood's Coins. The Author also considers the effects which a currency of this Copper money would have on the Trade and Manufactures of Ireland.
  The Author for a long time was supposed to be Deane Swift, and the Pamphlet was included in some of the Editions of his Works, but it is certainly not by him.

52. A New Dialogue Between Two *Beggars Upon the Passing of Wood's Coin. By M. B.
  Dublin. Printed, by G. N. in Crane-Lane, 1724.
  Sm. 8vo. 8 pp.
  Dix.

  During the Agitation in Parliament against the Coin. Asserts the great scarcity of small change, most of which consists of Raps. Hints that if the coins were made in Ireland from Irish copper, there would be less objection to them.

53. A Letter From a Quaker-Merch^t. To Will. Wood, Hard-Ware-Man.

> *Dublin : Printed by John Harding in Molesworth-Court in Fishamble-Street,* 1724.

> Sm. 8vo.   16 pp.

> *T.C.D.—R.R. pp.* 57.

Written after the investigation before the Privy Council in England. Quotes Fynes Morrison's History of Tyrone's Rébellion, for the exchange scheme tried to be worked in Ireland.

Says Wood has made four kinds of coin—Bad, Worse, Worst And Worst of All.   Signed Aminadab Firebrass.

54. Some farther Account Of The Original Disputes In Ireland, About Farthings and Halfpence.   In A Discourse With A Quaker of Dublin.........

> *Printed in the Year* 1724.

> 8vo.   47 pp.

> *B.M.* 1029, *b.* 26.

This Tract is written in defence of Wood, either by him or one in his employ, and is the only publication I have seen setting forth his side of the case.   It was no doubt circulated in Ireland, and in fact has the appearance of having been printed there.

55. Wood's Plot Discover'd By A Member of His Society; With His Apology to his Country-Men.

> *Dublin: Printed by G.N. opposite the Bear in Crane-Lane,* MDCCXXIV.

> Sm. 8vo.   13 pp. + 1 Adv.

> *B.M., C.* 58, *b.* 18.

Feigned to be written by John Brown, one of Wood's witnesses at the Council investigation.

Asserts that Wood has copper, brass and dirt mines.

Offers to make better money for 5d. a pound than Wood would sell for five groats.

No facts.   Scurrilous only.

The original owner of this Collection also attributed this Tract to Swift, practically because he makes use of a dirty expression in it.   It must be said, however, that there is nothing else of Swift in it.

56. A Letter To The Lord C——t, In Answer to some Arguments lately advanced in Favour of Mr. Wood's Copper Money.   By a Member of the Irish Parliament.........

> *Dublin: Printed by S. Powell, for George Ewin, Bookseller, at the Sign of the Angel and Bible in Dames-Street, over against the Castle Market,* 1724.

> 12mo.   16 pp. (dated Cork, Aug. 28, 1724).

> *H.C.*

Chiefly on the need for the money in Ireland, a fact which the Author entirely denies.   Also gives an account of John Brown's case in the House of Commons for conspiracy against John Bingham.   Seems Wood had correspondents in Ireland.   Says a Scotchman bought a quantity of Wood's money in Dublin the week before at a low price to disperse in his own country.   According to this Newton, the Controller of the Mint, was to get £2,800 from the Patent, and the Author insinuates that therefore he allowed Wood to put a few weighty half-pence into the Pyx in order to get a good report.

(21)

57. A Short Defence Of The People of Ireland, Occasion'd by the View Of A Letter from Mr. Wood, To one of the Managers Of His Copper Halfpence in Bristol. ....

Bristol: Printed, and Re-printed in Dublin by Pressick Rider, and Thomas Harbin, in the Exchange on Cork-Hill, 1724.

12mo. 8 pp.

U.C. Hib. 8, 724 (7).

Similar in style to the Drapier Letters. Accuses Wood of boasting that Walpole would soon be back in town and take such measures as to make the money pass. Asserts that Wood could not possibly be satisfied with £40,000, as it would mean no profit to him. Also there is no guarantee against foreigners making this coin.

58. Advice To The Roman Catholicks Of Ireland. Concerning Wood's Halfpence.

Dublin: Printed in the Year MDCCXXIV.

Sm. 8vo. 15 pp.

T.C.D.—Gall. A.A. 11, 24, *no.* 2.

Uses Wood's Halfpence as a text to preach against accepting trash of priestly coining.

59. Remarks Upon Mr. Wood's Coyn And Proceedings. Salus Populi, Suprema lex est. By Sir Michael Creagh.

Dublin: Printed by William Wilmot on the Blind-Key, 1724.

Sm. 8vo. 16 pp.

T.C.D.—Gall. A.A. 11, 24.

Claims the Committee, Newton, &c., were imposed upon, and that there is no doubt that the coins already brought to Ireland not only differ in weight materially, but also in fineness.

Besides the ordinary reasons advanced against the coin, it is the common notion in Ireland, that Ireland is regarded in England as an Eyesore, and that the People of England are very indifferent what becomes of the Trade and Commerce of Ireland, or what Disadvantages or Disasters may happen to it.

Suggests the great value of a Union with England to both Countries.

Speaks of William Wood having murdered poor Coward Wilson (probably in a Duel), and ruining many Thousands of Honest Men, Widows and Orphans.

Gilbert has some account of Sir Michael Creagh, from which it appears that he had a very curious career. He was Lord Mayor of Dublin in 1689, and took the part of James II in the ensuing War. He apparently went into exile, as he lived for seven years in Amsterdam, and in a Memorial to Lord Carteret of the 23 November, 1725, he petitioned for some recompense for his various losses and innocent sufferings.

This Tract seems to be unknown to Mason, or any of the writers on the Dispute about Wood's coinage.

60. A Word of Advice : Or, A Friendly Caution To the Collectors of Ireland, In Relation to Wood's Brass-Money.

Dublin: Printed by William Wilmot, on the Blind-Key, 1724.

Sm. 8vo. 15 pp. (signed Cato Ultonensis).

Dix.

Raises the legal doubt about the right of the Collectors of the Revenue to take anything except the current money of England, which brass counters not current in England are not. He based this on a Statute of 14 and 15 of Charles II, and asserts that Mr. Wood's Patent does not make the coins legal, and the Prerogative must give way to the Statute Law. Knox's Patent was on a different footing, because Knox was obliged to change his coin for gold and silver.

61. The Soldier's Plea : Against Mr. Wood's Brass-Money.
    Dublin : Printed by W. Wilmot. M.DCC.XXIV.
    Sm. 8vo. 8 pp.
    Dix.

Speaks of a Report that the Army is to be paid with Wood's Coin, the soldiers being obliged to pass it off for necessaries, or starve.

Appeals to the Statute of 14 and 15 of Charles II for protection against taking this Coin, until it be made current in England. The Patent left it to the choice of His Majestie's 'Subjects to receive or reject the Coin.

Evidently by the same author as "A Word of Advice or a Friendly Caution to the Collectors of Ireland."

62. Seasonable Advice to the Grand Jury respecting a Bill which is preparing for them to find against the printer of the Drapier's last letter.
    (*Dublin* 1724).
    Broadside dated Novem. 11. 1724.
    (By Jonathan Swift).
    T.C.D.—Press A. 7. 2. no. 76.

63. The Presentment Of The Grand-Jury Of The County of the City Of Dublin.
    (at end) *Dublin : Printed by Pressick Rider and Thomas Harbin at the General Office Printing-House in the Exchange, Cork-Hill,* 1724.
    Broadside.
    T.C.D.—Press A 7, 2. *no.* 89.

Presentment against the Coins, Nov. 28. 1724.

64. A Letter To the Right Honourable the Lord Viscount Molesworth. By M. B. Drapier, Author of the Letter to the Shop-Keepers, etc. ....
    Dublin : Printed by John Harding in Molesworth's Court in Fishamble-street.
    (The Fifth Letter). Dated Dec. 14, 1724.
    Sm. 8vo. 22 pp.
    (By Jonathan Swift).
    H.C.

Reprinted in all later editions of Swift.

65. Seasonable Advice To M. B. Drapier. Occasion'd by his Letter to the Right Honourable the Lord Viscount Molesworth.

    n. p. n. d. but probably 1724.

    Broadside, signed M. M.

    B.M. 2145. *h.* 1. (17)

Every Merchant in Dublin has got over his Window in large characters :—"I Won't Take Wood's Coin."

This very amusing skit appears to me to have been without doubt written by Swift himself.

66. The Fifth and Last Letter To the People of Ireland In Reference to Wood and his Brass.

    Dublin : Printed in the Year Mdccxxiv.

    Sm. 8vo. 14 pp. (Signed Hibernicus).

    B.M., C. 58. *b.* 18.

Give thanks for escaping the peril of Wood's coin to the "Loyal and true public-spirited Writings of some among us."

Thinks Wood's scheme was to draw away the specie to bring in the Pretender by furnishing him with our own money.

(No facts).

The original owner of this Collection in the British Museum attributes this Tract to Swift, but admits that it has never before appeared as his.

Probably by Sheridan.

67. The Sixth Letter To The Whole People Of Ireland. By An Ancient Patriot.

    Dublin : Printed in the Year 1724.

    Sm. 8vo. 15 pp. Signed Well Wisher.

    B.M., C. 58. *b.* 18.

This tract refers to the Brass money of James II and the rise of prices. Asserts the immense improvement of Ireland since that time, and speaks of the great increase of the population.

In spite of title not by Swift.

68. The Drapier Demolished And Set out in his own Proper Colours ; being a full Confutation of all his Arguments against Mr. Wood's Halfpence. By William Wood, Esq.

    (at end) *Dublin : Printed by John Harding in Molesworth's Court in Fishamble Street.*

    Sm. 8vo. 8 pp. (No regular title).

    B.M. 8133, *a* 10 (2).

Written 5 or 6 months after the first Drapier letter. Entirely ironical and reads very much like Swift's writing, and so ascribed in T.C.D. Collection.

69. The Funeral Of Wood's Halfpence A Sermon Preach'd against Coining of Base Money. By a Divine of the Church of England.

    Dublin : Printed by J. Carson, in Coghill's-Court, Dames-street, 1724.

    12mo. 22 pp.

    U.C. *Hib.* 8. 724. (7).

This is not a sermon, but a dissertation on money.

The above is the only copy I have seen.

70. A Letter From A Young Lady, To The Rev D—n S—t
....
   Printed in the Year 1724. (*Harding probably*).
   Sm. 8vo. 8 pp.
   Dix.
   Verses laudatory of Swift for his public spirit and call to action.

71. An Express from Elisium, To The Revd. Dr. M . . . . gu, Couple-Beggar, The only Way for W. Wood, to gain the Hearts of the unjustly irritated Hibernians, and make them receive, without Reluctancy : the Brass-Coin. With Advice how to Manage, (and some Observations on) M. B. Drapier. Written by the Late Famous Captain Fleming.
   Dublin, Printed in the Year 1724.
   Broadside.
   B.M. 8145 *h* 1 (11).
   A Squib suggesting that if Wood turned some brass into gold and threw some in the Drapier's eyes, or had him exalted one grade above the ascendant of St. Patrick's Steeple, that before the 10th of June he may change his tune.

72. Letter From Aminadab Firebrass Quaker Merchant, To M. B. Drapier.
   Dublin : Printed by John Harding in Molesworth's Court.
   Broadside Poem.
   T.C.D.—Press A. 7. 4. *no.* 129.

73. The Present State Of Ireland Consider'd : In a Letter to The Revd Dean Swift. By a True Patriot.
   Printed in the Year 1724.
   8 pp. Signed Hibernicus. (After the Drapier Letters, to which it refers).
   T.C.D.—P. pp. 15. *no.* 5.
   The author of this, who was probably Thomas Sheridan, complains bitterly about the Absentees and the commercial restrictions, especially the prohibition against exporting wool. He further complains about all the offices in Ireland being filled by Englishmen, and the dependent state of the Irish Parliament, which had no initiative in legislative matters.

74. The Truth of Some Maxims In State And Government, Examined With Reference to Ireland.
   Sir Henry Craik, in his Life of Swift, states incidentally that this Tract was published in 1724. But I think that this is probably an inadvertence, as—so far as I know—no copy of it exists, and it is usually reprinted from Deane Swift's Edition.

75. A Letter To M. B. Drapier. Author of a Letter to the Ld Molesworth, etc.
   ....
   Dublin : Printed in the Year 1724-5.
   8 sm. 8vo leaves. (Signed Misoxulos).
   Laudatory of the Drapier and his efforts, but without any economic value.

76. Woods Reviv'd Or, A Short Defence Of His Proceedings In Bristol, London, etc. In Reference To The Kingdom Of Ireland.

> *Printed in the Year* 1724-5.
> Sm. 8vo. 14 pp.
> *B.M., C.* 58 *b* 18.

Ironical pamphlet signed Will. Wood.

Speaks of the Patent being laid just now before the Council. Sets forth his villainy, and says he set out to cheat the people of Ireland, on the advice of some renegade Irishmen.

In the style of Swift, but an imitation only.

From the contents it would appear to have been written in 1724.

At the end of the volume in the British Museum, in which this Tract is bound, appears some manuscript notes in which it is stated that this never appeared in any edition of Swift, until Sir Walter Scott gave it in his through the kindness of Mr. Barrett. The collector appeared to consider it as undoubtedly by Swift.

Not reprinted by Temple Scott.

77. His Excellency John Lord Carteret Lord Lieutenant General and General Governor of Ireland, His Speech to both Houses of Parliament at Dublin : On Tuesday the Twenty First Day of September, 1725.

> (at end) *Dublin : Printed by Andrew Crooke, &c.* 1725.
> Broadside.
> *B.M.* 8145. *h.* 1. (21).

Announces that an entire end is put to the Patent, formerly granted to Mr. Wood.

Original (T.C.D. Press A. 7.2. 90) in 4 folio Pages with a regular title.

78. On Wisdom's Defeat In a Learned Debate. Quod est Sapiente semper idem velle, atq; idem nolle.

> 4 stanzas. Begins :—" Minerva has vow'd since the Bishops do slight
> Signed Rose Common,
> Shameless Woman "
> (at end) *Dublin : Printed by Sarah Harding on the Blindkey.* (*n. d.* but 1725).
> *National Library, Dublin.*

Sarah Harding was voted into custody by Parliament for printing this skit.

79. The Case Of John Browne Esq ;

> *London : Printed in the Year* M.DCC.XXV.
> Sm. 4to. 16 pp.
> *H.C.*

Browne wrote this Tract probably in consequence of the attacks made on him by Swift, in the Third Drapier Letter.

He claims that having been forced to leave Ireland on account of the unjust prosecution against him by the House of Commons, he took refuge in London. While frequenting the Coffee-houses he had stated that there was a demand for a reasonable supply of copper-coins in Ireland. This coming to the ears of Wood, he had been summoned to appear before the Committee of Inquiry and voted into custody, and thus obliged to give evidence.

He also defends himself against a charge of having issued Tickets or Tallies to Workmen in his Works in Ireland. He admits that he had done so, but claimed that they had all been redeemed. He afterwards wrote a letter to Swift, justifying himself and complaining of Swift's attacks on him. It is dated April 4th, 1728, and is printed in vol. VII in Sir Walter Scott's Edition of Swift. Browne wrote several pamphlets of considerable importance on Economic Affairs in Ireland, and altogether was a man of considerable importance, being afterwards knighted.

Browne had a small Iron-Works in County Mayo.

80. A Letter From A Clergy-Man In the Country, To H. R. Esq; a Member of Parliament, in the City.
   (at end) *Printed in the Year* 1725.
   2 folio sheets.
   B.M. 8145. *h.* 1. (23).

Gives a woeful picture of Dublin and speaks of the increase of profanity, lewdness and debauchery, ale-houses, frauds in drugs, increase of attornies and pettifoggers, adulteration of wine. False weights and measures were used not only by the merchants, but also by the bankers, money-changers and usurers. There was a flood of foolish pamphlets, obscene ballads, and romantick books.

The author recommends a duty on plate in Ireland, and deals with the scarcity of small silver, suggesting that his Majesty be addressed for coining small silver.

81. Methods Proposed for Regulating The Poor, Supporting of Some and Employing Others, according to their several Capacities. By Sir W. F. [*i.e.* Sir William Fownes].
   Dublin : Printed by and for J. Hyde, Bookseller in Dame's Street, 1725.
   8vo. 16 pp.
   Dix.

A Proposal for Badges for the Poor, distinctive for each Parish or City, the less incapable to be employed in repairing the roads.

Evidently the wandering Poor were a great grievance, but according to this, there were regular bands going about especially in summer, and the Farmers found them necessary for harvest-work.

Fownes, the Author, was an Alderman of Dublin, and at one time Lord Mayor.

82. Enquiries Into The Principal Causes Of The General Poverty Of The Common People of Ireland. With Remedies Propos'd for Removing of them. ....
   Dublin : Printed and Sold by George Faulkner, in Pembroke-Court, Castle-Street, M.DCC.XXV.
   8vo. 25 pp.
   T.C.D.—P. pp. 7, *no.* 16.

The chief trouble is scarcity of money and small share of private credit among dealers. Compares Dutch traders with Irish with interest at 3 per cent. instead of 7 per cent., as legal in Ireland.

Estimates Linen and Yarn trade at £600,000 yearly. The Husband-men, Tradesmen, and other industrious and laborious People need to have small sums of Money at easy rates of interest. "Money is the Tools with which industrious Men must work." Suggests Lombards.

This Tract may be imperfect, as there is an hiatus in the text between pp. 16-17, although signatures and paging agree. Also branches off into a discussion of the Law abuses on p. 17.

83. Fraud Detected : Or, The Hibernian Patriot. Containing, All the Drapier's Letters to the People of Ireland, on Wood's Coinage, &c. Interspers'd with the following Particulars, viz.:

I. The Addresses of the Lords and Commons of Ireland, against Wood's Coin.

II. His Majesty's Answer to the said Addresses.

III. The Report of his Majesty's most honourable Privy Council.

IV. Seasonable Advice to the Grand Jury.

V. Extract of the Votes of the House of Commons of England, upon breaking a Grand Jury.

VI. Considerations on the Attempts made to pass Wood's Coin.

VII. Reasons, shewing the Necessity the People of Ireland are under, to refuse Wood's Coinage.

To which are added, Prometheus. A Poem. Also a new Poem to the Drapier ; and the Songs Sung at the Drapier's Club in Truck Street, Dublin, never before printed. With a Preface, explaining the Usefulness of the Whole.

Dublin : Re-printed and Sold by George Faulkner in Pembroke-Court, Castle-street, 1725.

Sm. 8vo, 14, 222 and 2 pp.

First collected edition of the Drapier Letters, including two of David Bindon's, Nos. VI and VII.

Second edition in 1730.

84. The Present State Of The Tillage in Ireland, Considered, And Some Methods offered For its Improvement. By S. P. ......

Dublin : Printed by George Grierson, at the Two Bibles in Essex-Street. MDCCXXV.

(By S. Pierson).

35 pp. b. t. 1 plate.

85. Tables Of Exchange. In Two Parts.

Part First. English Money Exchanged into Irish, etc. etc.

Part Second. Irish Money Exchanged into English, etc. etc.

Dublin : Printed for John Watson, Bookseller on the Merchants-Key near the Old Bridge, by J. Gowan in Back-Lane, 1727.

12mo. 2 pp. Ded. to James Swift, 2 Pref. of Explanation, balance tables without pagination.

Interesting because it contains in the front a page of bankers and merchants, who approve the book, and at the end 5 pp. of subscribers.

86. Proposals For A Publick Coinage Of Copper Half-pence and Farthings In The Kingdom of Ireland, Of The Copper ore or Mine thereof, for the Common Benefit, both of the Crown and Nation, to the Increase of 254297 Pound Ster. of Gold and Silver Specie.

    By James Maculla, Pewterer and Artificer in Metals.

    Dublin : Printed by J. Gowan at the Spinning-Wheel in Back Lane. 1727.

    8vo. 21 pp. b. t.

    T.C.D.—Gall. L. 3. 45. *no.* 3.

87. A Short View Of The State Of Ireland.

    Dublin : Printed by S. Harding, next Door to the Crown in Copper-Alley, 1727-8.

    Sm. 8vo. 15 pp.

    (By Jonathan Swift).

    B.M. 8145. *a.* 28.

    Reprinted in the Intelligencer as No. 15.

88. *The Lamentable- Cry of the People of Ireland to Parliament.* A Coinage, or Mint, Proposed. The Parliament of Ireland's Address, And The King's Answer thereunto, Relating To The Coining Copper Half-Pence and Farthings For this Nation. With Several Reasons and Observations, Shewing The great Necessity there is for such a Coin; and a Scheme laid Down, demonstrating that the Nation will have an Increase in Cash, as well Gold and Silver, as Copper Money, of Two Hundred and Fifty Thousand Pounds, sterl. by means thereof : And that the said Summ may be deemed all Profit to the Kingdom. By James Maculla of the City of Dublin, Artificer in divers Mettals, viz. Pewter, Brass, and Copper, etc.

    Dublin : Printed by Edward Waters, 1728.

    Sm. 4to. 11 pp.

    B.M. 8225. *bb.* 62.

States that he has just published a paper, entitled "Proposals for a Publick Coinage of Half-pence and Farthings in the Kingdom of Ireland." The copper coinage in use is adulterated with lead and counterfeit, so that its intrinsic value is only one-sixth of what it passes for.

Also hints that Wood's scheme had been really a mining scheme to find a market for the English copper they proposed to mine, and thinks that he was the earliest person that discovered the ill consequences it might have had in this Kingdom.

The Author's scheme is for a manufacture of copper coinage in Ireland from Irish Copper from Irish Mines, the same to be of the same weight, value, perfection and goodness as the English Copper Coinage.

Calculated that they could work up an export trade in them to the plantations at a profit of 9 per cent. in exchange.

Calculated one million in silver plate in Ireland.

£20,000 yearly of Tin imported to Ireland.

Applied for the Coinage himself, which he estimates will give the Nation a profit of 20 per cent.

Swift wrote an answer to this project, entitled "A Letter on Mr. M'Culla's Project About Halfpence, and a New one Proposed." It does not seem to have been printed at the time, but appears in the later editions of Swift's Works.

Maculla actually entered on the Manufacture of these Coins, which were made in the form of Promissory Notes.

89. Seasonable Remarks On Trade. With Some Reflections on the Advantages that might accrue to Great Britain, by a proper Regulation of the Trade of Ireland. Wrote in London, but now first Publish'd in Dublin, as a Preface to other Essays on the Trade and Manufactures of Ireland.

Dublin : Printed by S. Powell, for George Ewing, at the Angel and Bible in Dame's-street, MDCCXXVIII.

8vo. Tit. 6 Ded. to Lord Carteret. 70 pp.

(By John Browne).

B.M. 8245 *b* 92 (1)

Forms No. 1 of a Collection of Tracts concerning the Present State of Ireland, printed in London, 1729.

This Tract written while Browne was in England, is a plea to the English Nation to relax some of the restrictions on Irish trade, and especially to encourage the shipping interest there. The author gives a sketch of the history of trade, the rise of the Dutch, and foretells their approaching fall.

90. A Letter To the Author of the Short View Of The State of Ireland.

By the Author of Seasonable Remarks.

Dublin : Printed and Sold by S. Powell, in Copper-Alley, near Cork-Hill. 1728.

8vo. 16 pp.

(By John Browne).

H.C. 81.

91. An Essay On Trade in General; And, on that of Ireland in Particular. By the Author of Seasonable Remarks.

Dublin : Printed by S. Powell, for George Ewing, at the Angel and Bible in Dame's-street, 1728.

8vo. Tit. 10 Ded. to Speaker Conelly, 3 Index, 119 pp.

(By John Browne).

B.M. 8245 *b* 92 (2)

Forms No. 2 of Collection of Tracts concerning Present State of Ireland.

After giving an account of trade in general, written in the true Mercantile spirit, the author proceeds to give a history of English trade monopolies, and the restrictions on Irish trade, ending with a comprehensive survey of the trade of the world at large.

92. Considerations On Two Papers Lately Published, The First, called, Seasonable Remarks, etc. And the other, An Essay on Trade in General, and on That of Ireland, in Particular.

Dublin : Printed in the Year 1728.

8vo.   16 pp.

B.M. 8245 *aaa* 3.

Forms No. 3 of Collection of Tracts concerning Present State of Ireland.
(Another edition, 1729).

This Tract was supposed by Browne to have been written by Swift and answered in " A Reply to the Observer, etc." but this seems to me unlikely, and I believe it to have been written by Arthur Dobbs.

The author disputes Browne's facts and opinions about the increase of wealth in Ireland in the preceding fifty years, and denies the alleged profitable nature of the trade with France.

93. A Reply To the Observer on Seasonable Remarks.
  Dublin : Printed by S. Powell, and Sold by George Ewing at the Angel and Bible in Dame's-street, MDCCXXVIII.
  8vo.   Tit. 16 Ded. to Swift.   31 pp.
  (Probably by John Browne).
  B.M. 8245. *b.* 92 (3).

94. An Appeal To the Revd. Dean Swift, By way of Reply To the Observer on Seasonable Remarks. ... .
  Dublin : Printed and Sold by S. Powell, in Copper-Alley, near Cork-Hill. 1728.
  8vo.   16 pp.
  (By John Browne).
  T.C.D.—P. pp. 15. *no.* 6.

No. 4 of Collection of Tracts concerning the present state of Ireland.

95. A Letter In Answer To a Paper, intitled, An Appeal To the Reverend Dean Swift.   By the Author of Considerations on Two Papers, &c.   ....
  Dublin : Printed by and for Thomas Hume, at the Custom-House Printing-House in Essex-street, 1728.
  8vo.   16 pp.
  T.C.D.—P. ii. 25. *no.* 7.

Forms no. 5 of Collection of Tracts concerning the Present State of Ireland.
By the same author as 92, probably Arthur Dobbs.

96. The Memorial to the R—d. J—n S—t, of the poor inhabitants, tradesmen, and labourers of the Kingdom of Ireland. Presented by Thomas Walsh, Skinner's Row.
  12mo.

The title of this Tract, which I have never seen, is taken from Madden's " History of the Irish Periodical Literature."

There seems to be no doubt that this is the original of Sir John Browne's Tract, answered by Swift, at least the one usually ascribed to Browne, although I do not find anything in other works by Browne to indicate that he wrote the Memorial.

(31)

97. An Answer To A Paper, Called A Memorial Of the Poor Inhabitants, Tradesmen and Labourers of the Kingdom of Ireland. By the Author of the Short View of the State of Ireland. *Dublin: Printed by S. Harding, next Door to the Crown in Copper-Alley,* 1728.
 Sm. 8vo. Dated March 25th, 1728. 16 pp.
 (By Jonathan Swift).
 T.C.D.—R.R. m.m. 65 *no.* 17.

Swift objects to the memorialist's scheme for giving a premium of £10,000 for bringing in £100,000 worth of corn, the same to be paid for by taxing some imported luxuries. It would be better to propose a general contribution to support the poor with potatoes and buttermilk.
Reprinted in 1738, and in all late editions of Swift.

98. The Humble Representation Of The House of Commons To The King, With His Majesty's Most Gracious Answer Thereunto. *Dublin: Printed by and for Thomas Hume, at the Custom-House Printing-House in Essex-Street, over-against Essex-Bridge,* 1728.
 8vo. 16 pp.
 H.C. 81.

Account of the Finances, &c.

99. Farther Considerations For The Improvement Of The Tillage In Ireland. With An Account of the Advantages of the Ploughs and Methods recommended in a former Treatise, as since proved on Tryal. And Some Remarks added for an easy Improvement of the Lands now used in Tillage, and of other Lands in this Kingdom. By Sam. Pierson, A.B. ......
 Dublin: Printed by George Grierson at the Two Bibles in Essex-Street. MDCCXXVIII.
 8vo. 42 pp.

100. Some Thoughts Concerning Government in General : And Our Present Circumstances On Great Britain and Ireland. ....
 Dublin: Printed by and for J. Hyde, Bookseller in Dames-Street. MDCCXXVIII.
 8vo. 60 pp.
 H.C. 81.

Another edition of this was issued, dated 1731, the same as above except that it had by " A. D." on the title (probably Arthur Dobbs).

101. The Intelligencer. Numb. 1.
 Saturday. May 11, To be Continued Weekly.
 Dublin: Printed by S. Harding, next Door to the Crown in Copper-Alley, 1728.
 8vo.
 H.C. (12 numbers only, but 20 printed).
 19 Numbers were reprinted in London together as :—

The Intelligencer. ....

Printed at Dublin. London Reprinted, and sold by A. Moor in St. Paul's Church-yard, and the Booksellers of London and Westminster. MDCCXXIX.

8vo. Tit., 2 pp. to the Reader, 2 Conts., 217 pp. 19 numbers.

It was published as a weekly paper in Dublin in 1728 and 1729 by Swift and Sheridan.

Swift's Letter to Pope, 12th June, 1731, gives authorship as follows:—Swift, Nos. 1, 3, 5, 7, verses of 8, 9, verses of 10, 15, 19.

Sheridan wrote the others.

No. 15 is a Reprint of "Short View of the State of Ireland," written late in 1727.

No. 19 also written before.

Monck Mason, in his History of St. Patrick, says that he had 20 original numbers, of which the last was a double number, one part evidently by Swift.

No. 6 is on the "Poverty of Ireland," also no. 17.

102. Reflections Little to the Purpose, On A Paper Less to the Purpose. By the Author of Seasonable Remarks. ......

Dublin : Printed by S. Powell, and Sold by G. Ewing, at the Angel and Bible in Dame's-street, E. Hamilton, at the Corner of Christ-Church-Lane, High-street, and J. Watson, on the Merchants-Key near the Old Bridge, 1729.

Sm. 8vo, viii + 56.

(By Sir John Browne).

B.M. 8245 *b* 91 (2).

Another edition same year in viii + 72 pp.

An answer to 95.

103. An Essay On The Gold and Silver-Coin Currant In Ireland. By Mr. Bindon. ...

Dublin : Printed by E. Dobson, at the Stationers-Arms in Castle-Street, MDCCXXIX.

Tit. Ded. 28 pp. + 3 Tables.

B.M. 1139 *K.* 6 (3).

104. A List Of The Absentees Of Ireland, And The Yearly Value of their Estates and Incomes spent abroad. With Observations On The Present State and Condition Of That Kingdom.

....

Dublin: Printed for R. Gunne in Capel-street. MDCCXXIX

8vo. 1 Ded. to Lord Carteret. 80 pp.

(By Thomas Prior).

Thomas Prior died October 21, 1751, and a short obituary notice—without, however, giving any facts of his life—appeared in "The Dublin Weekly Journal" of October 22.

The D.P.E. gives a short account of Prior's writings especially this one, which formed the basis of many subsequent works on Ireland. It is plain there is something wrong with the calculations, but the evils of absenteeism impressed every one who lived in Ireland or investigated its economic difficulties.

105. The Case Of the Poor of the Kingdom of Ireland, Stated and Considered upon the common Principles of Christianity.
(at end) *Dublin: Printed for William Smith, at the Hercules in Dame's Street, Bookseller,* 1729.
Broadside (not by Swift).
T.C.D.—Press A. 7, 5, *no.* 128.

106. Considerations On The Act For Encouraging In-land Navigation In Ireland. With Some Hints of a Method for Enforcing and Executing that Act. In A Letter From A Country Gentleman to his Friend in the House of Commons.
Dublin: Printed in the Year MDCCXXIX.
8vo. 74 pp.
H.C. 86.

107. A Letter To The People Of Ireland. By M. B. Draper ....
Dublin: Printed and sold by Thomas Hume, at the Custom-House Printing-House in Essex-street, 1729.
8vo. 16 pp. Signed Publicola.
H.C. 85.

108. The Case Of Many Thousand poor Inhabitants of Dublin: In a Letter to a worthy Member of Parliament, concerning the extravagant Rates and Price of Coals, in the City, with a Recommendation for the importing Kilkenny-Coals here, from Ross and Waterford and other Ports of this Kingdom.
The second Impression with a Postscript, by M. B., dated May 28, 1729.
12mo. 8 pp.
(at end) *Dublin: Printed by Christopher Dickson, in the Post-Office-yard in Sycamore-Alley,* 1729.
H.C. 87.

This Tract originally appeared in "The Dublin Weekly Journal" of August 9, 1729, and was dated August 4, 1729. It is reprinted in Scott's Swift (Vol. VII) with a note in which the Editor thinks "that the composition, though very careless, retains very strong marks of the Dean's peculiar style." These remarks also apply to the second letter, and "The Further Case," which appeared in "The Dublin Weekly Journal" of August 16, and which was also reprinted separately.

109. A Supplement To The Drapier's Letter in the Behalf of many Thousand poor Inhabitants of this City. Or, A Third Letter, in Answer to a worthy Member of Parliament. Concerning the Extravagant Rates, and Price of Coals, with a Recommendation, for the importing Kilkenny-Coals, from Ross, Waterford, and other Ports of this Kingdom.
Dated Sept. 23, 1729.
8vo. 8 pp.
H.C. 87.

This Supplement was printed in "The Dublin Weekly Journal" of October 25, but Scott does not think that Swift was the author of this.

(34)

110. Remarks on the Scheme For Supplying the City of Dublin with Coals from the County of Tyrone. In a Letter to Thomas Burgh Esq; His Majesty's Engineer and Surveyor-General.
12mo. 7 pp.
(By Francis Seymour).
H.C. 87.

111. Animadversions on Several Proposals Now under Consideration, for Supplying of the City of Dublin with Coals, &c.
8vo. 7 pp.
H.C. 87.

112. The Benefits Which arise to a Trading People From Navigable Rivers. To which are added, some Considerations On the Origin of Loughs and Bogs ; and a Scheme, for the establishment of a Company, to make the River Shannon navigable, humbly offered to the Publick. By John Browne, Esq ; Author of the Seasonable Remarks, of the Essay upon Trade, of the Scheme of the Money-Matters of Ireland, and of several other Pamphlets, upon the Affairs of this Country.
Dublin : Printed by S. Powell, and Sold by George Ewing, at the Angel and Bible in Dames's-street, E. Hamilton, at the Corner of Christ-Church-lane, High-street, and J. Watson, on the Merchants-Key, near the Old-Bridge, Bookseller, MDCCXXIX.
8vo. VI—45—8vo.
B.M. 8245, *b.* 91 (1).

Proposes creating a company with £11,000 stock to do this work, and that a Bank be created by the Governors at the headquarters at Athlone, issuing notes and buying Exchange.

113. A Second Letter To A Member of Parliament Recommending the Improvement Of The Irish Fishery.
Dublin : Printed by A. Rhames, opposite the Pied-Horse in Capel-street, MDCCXXIX.
8vo. 30 pp.
H. C. 87.

114. Observations On Coin In General With Some Proposals For Regulating the Value of Coin In Ireland.
By the Author of the List of the Absentees of Ireland [*i.e.,* Thomas Prior].
Dublin : Printed by A. Rhames, for R. Gunne in Castle-Street, MDCCXXIX.
8vo. 64 pp.
B.M. 104, *f.* 16.

Reprinted by the Political Economy Club, with a preface by M'Culloch, 1856, in a select collection. D. P. E. also gives some account of this tract.

115. A Modest Proposal For preventing the Children Of Poor People
From being a Burthen to their Parents, Or The Country, And
For making them Beneficial to the Publick.
> *Dublin : Printed by S. Harding, opposite the Hand and
> Pen near Fishamble-Street, on the Blind Key.* MDCCXXIX.
> Sm. 8vo. 16 pp.
> By Jonathan Swift.
> *T.C.D.—P. pp.* 15, *no.* 9.

Many other Editions, and reprinted in all late Editions of Swift's
Works.
This is one of the most famous pamphlets that was ever written.

116. An Essay On The Trade And Improvement Of Ireland.
> By Arthur Dobbs, Esq.
> *Dublin: Printed by A. Rhames, for J. Smith and W. Bruce
> on the Blind-Key.* MDCCXXIX.
> 8vo. 99 pp.

An Essay On The Trade Of Ireland.   Part II.
By Arthur Dobbs, Esq.
> *Dublin:* Same, MDCCXXIX
> 8 Ded. to Duke of Dorset.   147 pp. + 1 Errata.

Second Part of this famous book.
Dobbs' name appears in the D. N. B., and a short account of his career
with a reference to this book is given by Palgrave in the D. P. E.

117. A Collection Of Tracts, Concerning the Present State of Ireland, With Respect to its Riches, Revenue, Trade, and Manufactures.   Containing
> I. Seasonable Remarks on Trade. &c.
> II. An Essay on Trade in General ; and on that of Ireland in Par-
> ticular.
> III. Considerations on two Papers lately published (Swift).
> IV. An Appeal to the Reverend Dean Swift by way of Reply to
> above.
> V. A Letter in Answer to a Paper intitl'd, an Appeal, &c.

> *London : Printed for S. Woodward and J. Peele*.........
> MDCCXXIX.
> False and Full Title.   144 pp.   8vo.   Separate Title-pages
> to each tract, all dated 1729.
> A collection of nos. 89, 91, 92, 94 and 95.
> *B.M.* 884, *h.* 12 (2).

118. A Scheme For Supplying Industrious Men with Money To
carry on their Trades, And for better Providing for the Poor
of Ireland.   The second Edition.
> *Dublin : Printed by Thomas Hume, opposite Essexbridge,
> in Essex-street.* 1729.
> 8vo.   22 pp. + 2 Tables.
> By David Bindon.
> *B.M.* 8282, *b.* 23.
> Second Edition, same and same year.

Third Edition, by Faulkner, in 1750, in 27 pp., sm. 8vo, with a short Preface.

Bindon's name appears signed to the Dedication to Lord Carteret.

He proposes a system of municipal Lombards in Ireland, loaning at rates of from 10 per cent. to 20 per cent., according to the amount of the loan. It seems the rate of interest at the Amsterdam Lombard was 16¾ per cent. for sums under 100 florins, which, considering the relative rates in both countries, he thinks much higher than the 20 per cent. he proposes on a similar class of loan.

119. A Short Account Of The Reasons Of The Intended Alteration Of The Value of the Coins Currant in this Kingdom.
    Dublin : Printed by A. Rhames—MDCCXXIX.
    8vo. 8 pp.
    B.M. 1139, *K.* 6 (4).
    Another edition printed by A. Rhames, same year, with a different Title-page.
    8vo. 8 pp.

This Tract was probably written by Mr. Maple, the supposed author of "The Vindication of the Intended Alterations."

The Government, after receiving the application of the principal gentlemen in the country, have endeavoured to remedy the inconveniences complained of by the new Regulations, which the preceding summer were communicated to the merchants and remitters, who immediately raised a clamour against them.

The object of this paper is to defend the Government proposals which, briefly, were to regulate the gold coins according to their current value in England. Under this a guinea would pass for 21s. English, or 22s. 9d. Irish; a Moidore for 29s. 3d. Irish, and so on. For foreign silver the Mexico piece of Eight of 17 dwts. 4 gr. to be the standard, and valued at 5s. Irish. At this rate foreign silver would pass at 5s. 9d. 3 qr. ·611 per oz., which falls a little short of the usual price of bullion in Ireland, namely 5s. 10d.

120. A Scheme Of the Money-Matters Of Ireland. In which the Consequences of raising or lowering the Coin, are impartially consider'd............
    Dublin : Printed by S. Powell, and Sold by G. Ewing, at the Angel and Bible in Dame's-street ; MDCCXXIX.
    Ded. to Sir Ralph Gore.
    8vo. 57 pp. (pp. 21, 22, 31, 32 each double pages of Tables).
    By Sir John Browne.
    B.M. 1139, *K.* 6 (2).

Another edition, same year, identical with this, except Imprint.

A general description of money and its functions, followed by an examination of the state of the circulation of Ireland, in which he finds only £14,000 in silver and copper, to circulate £900,000 of gold and paper.

Then examines the project of reducing the value of the money circulating in Ireland. The coins circulating are all under-valued, except the large new Portugal gold coins.

His scheme is to raise the silver instead of reducing the gold.

121. A Vindication Of the Intended Alterations Of The Value of the several Coins Now Currant in this Kingdom From the Objections made against them.

> *Dublin : Printed by A. Rhames,* MDCCXXIX.
> 8vo. 54 pp.
> *B.M.* 1139, *K.* 6 (5).

Browne, in "A Short Review of the several Pamphlets," says this tract is by M—ple, *i.e.*, Maple, a chemist, of Dublin.

A more detailed account of the proceedings taken to change the value of the current coin, which began as early as 1725.

One very sound argument against any scheme which would introduce English silver, was the illegality of exporting it, while with the present currency of foreign coin they had practically a free market for coin.

The tract is an answer to Bindon's and Browne's Observations on the matter, and the author also denies the many alleged advantages of a Mint for Ireland.

The author had appeared before the Council and vigorously advocated the reduction of the gold, according to Browne, who, in his "Short Review" (1730), violently attacked this pamphlet and its supposed author, Mr. Maple.

122. The Tribune. To be continued Weekly. Numb. I. Tuesday Oct. 7th. 1729.

> *Dublin : Printed for and Sold by S. Powell,* 1729.
> *H.C.* 88.

No. 21 is the last given here (all published).

Written chiefly by Sheridan and Dr. Delany.

Nos. 17 and 18 give an account of the state of the peasantry ; nos. 6, 7, 9 and 10 deal with the trade and manufactures of Ireland.

The Tribune was reprinted in London and sold by Warner, MDCCXXIX, with some poems added in 172 pp. (b.t.) + 4 pp. contents.

123. A Letter to the people of Ireland, relating to the copper half-pence coining in Dublin, shewing that this nation will gain £100,000 sterling cash by the same.

> *Printed by E. Waters.*
> 12mo.

The title of this Tract, which I have not seen, is taken from Madden's "History of Irish Periodical Literature."

It is apparently one of Maculla's effusions, and no doubt refers to his private coinage of Copper Tokens. It is, therefore, probably of the date 1729.

124. A Short Review Of the several Pamphlets that have appeared this Session On The Subject of Coin, And in particular of that which is intitl'd, "A Vindication Of the Intended Alterations Of The Value of the several Coins now currant in this Kingdom From the Objections made against them."

> *Dublin. Powell,* MDCCXXX.
> 8vo. 48 pp.
> By Sir John Browne.
> *B.M.* 1139, *K.* 6 (6).

Another edition same year, with different title-page.

In this tract Browne reviews the controversy, approving of Bindon's arguments and a part of Prior's, but vigorously attacks the "Vindication of the Intended Alterations." Nothing was accomplished at this time, but the Government was persistent, and in 1737 succeeded in reducing the value of the gold coins.

Swift was violently opposed to this plan, largely basing his opinion on the supposed advantage which the Absentees would draw from the lowering, and, indeed, this seems to have been the most popular objection. The change was carried through by the Primate, Hugh Boulter, in whose letters will be found many references to the matter.

125. A List Of The Absentees Of Ireland, and The Yearly Value of their Estates and Incomes spent abroad. With Observations On The Present Trade and Condition of that Kingdom.

The Second Edition; Corrected. To which is added, A Large Appendix, containing a farther List and Observations. *London : Printed for Weaver Bickerton*, M.DCC.XXX.

....

8vo. 1 Ded. 2 Pref. 94 pp. + 1 (Order of House of Commons).

By Thomas Prior.

126. The Present State of Ireland Consider'd.

Dublin: Printed by and for George Grierson, MDCCXXX.
8vo. XV pp.-80.

"The Present State" was also reprinted same year in London for Weaver Bickerton.

32 pp.

B.M. 1029, *e.* 14.

A reprint of the " List of Absentees " by Prior, with a preface prefixed.

127. Remarks on Some Maxims, Peculiar to the Ancient as well as Modern Interests of Ireland. With a Seasonable Hint to G— B—n about the Woollen Trade.

In a Letter from a Gentleman in the County of Kerry, to his Friend in Dublin.

Dublin: Printed in the Year 1730.
8vo. 8 pp.
H.C. 98.

128. The Hibernian Patriot: Being a Collection of the Drapier's Letters To the People of Ireland, Concerning Mr. Wood's Brass Half-pence. Together with Considerations On The Attempts made to pass that Coin And Reasons for the People of Ireland's refusing it.

To which are added Poems and Songs relating to the same subject.

Printed at Dublin. London—reprinted by A. Moor, etc., MDCCXXX.

8vo. 264 pp.

Second edition of the collection.

The Preface contains a slight account of the controversy copied from

Faulkner's edition, with some remarks on the " Seasonable Advice to the Grand Jury " inserted.

Also inserted is a poem, " To the Worthy Author of the Drapier's Letters, by a Youth of Fourteen Years of Age," and added a poem entitled " Drapier's Hill."

Otherwise a copy of Faulkner's edition of 1725.

129. Reflections Upon the Present unhappy Circumstances Of Ireland; In A Letter To His Grace the Lord Arch Bishop of Cashel. With a Proposal for Publick Granaries, as the principal Means whereby to retrieve our Affairs.

Dublin: Printed by George Faulkner, M,DCC,XXXI.
8vo.   37 pp.   Signed John Browne at end.
H.C.

130. Reasons For Regulating The Coin, And reducing the Interest; With a Scheme for paying part of the National Debt without burthening Ireland.

Printed in the Year 1731.   [*Dublin.*]
8vo.   24 pp.
H.C.

Proposes reducing Irish money to the English values.

More money in the country than 20 or 30 years before, and the country commodities bring better prices. Raising and lowering the coin of no importance, provided all different kinds be raised or lowered in the same proportions. As it stands now all coin is brought in in moidores and taken out in English silver or Guineas, and the loss to the country is the difference in the values of these abroad. Changing the value of the coin chiefly affects people with fixed incomes.

Proposes reducing Interest to 5 per cent. or 6 per cent.

The present irregularities of the coin enable Bankers and foreign merchants to make a profit by simply carrying over one kind of money and bringing another back. Gives an abstract of trade.

In Dublin rarely can a Trader or Manufacturer borrow under 10 per cent. although on real security interest is 5½ or 6 per cent. National Debt about £330,000.

131. Reflections On The National Debt; With Reasons For Reducing the Legal Interest; And against a Publick Loan. With Some Advice to the Electors of Members of Parliament.

Printed in the Year 1731.   [*Dublin.*]
8vo.   16 pp.
B.M. 8145 *a* 29.

Objects to the Borough System and says only resident Burgesses and Freemen should have a right to vote.

Also objects to a new loan, because the M.P.'s lend the money, and thus become Pensioners of the Court.

The placemen are getting Dispensations from the payment of 4 per cent. in the pound when absent.

For some time it has been mooted to reduce the rate of interest to 6 per cent., which he approves of. Now people put away their money, hoping to lend it to the public.

(Interest was reduced to 6 per cent. in 1732).

132. A Letter To A Member of Parliament, Upon the Deficiency of the Funds and Increase of the Debt, with an humble Proposal to raise a Fund to Pay it.
    By a Gentleman in the Country.
    Dublin: Printed in the Year MDCCXXXI.
    8vo. 15 pp. Signed Philopatris.
    H.C. 100.
    Proposes to stop smuggling, and suggests a regulated Poll-Tax graduated.

133. A Letter from A Gentleman In the Country To A Member of Parliament.
    Dublin: Faulkner. MDCCXXXI.
    8vo. 13 pp.
    Dix.
    On Mines.

134. King George And His Ancestors Parliamentary Grants To The People Of Ireland, Fairly Explained, For the manufacturing Copper change therein, by Virtue of the Laws, Grants, and Statutes of this Kingdom, and by Vertue of the Grants as aforesaid, £40,000 of Parliament Half-pence, are speedily to be manufactured for this Nation.
    Dublin: Printed by George Faulkner 1731.
    Written by James Maculla, Metallist and Parliamentary Manufacturer of Copper change.
    8vo. 35 pp.
    T.C.D.—P. pp. 21 *no.* 10.
    Proposal to issue half-pence of the English standard in form of promissory notes, James Maculla manufacturer's name on coin and promise to pay 20/- in the Pound, all to be from Farthings to Sixpenny pieces (Notes he calls them). Claims the laws permitted this, and the statutes cited certainly warranted his contention.
    Seems to imply that some of these were struck off, which as a matter of fact was the case.

135. An Inquiry Into Some of the Causes Of the Ill Situation of the Affairs Of Ireland. ......
    Dublin: Printed by Geo. Grierson, M,DCC,XXX,I.
    8vo. 39 pp.
    Although this Tract is based on Prior's List of Absentees, it is evidently by another author.

136. The Drapier Reviv'd : Or Considerations on the Inconvenience which the People of Ireland labour under for the Want of Small Change ; with the Reason thereof ; and a modest Proposal to remedy the same.
    By J. B. Esq ; [Probably John Browne].
    Dublin: Printed in the Year 1731.
    12mo. 8 pp.
    H.C. 101.
    This is the same argument, and, indeed, the same words to some extent as "Some Observations on the Present Currency, as well as the Intrinsick Value of the Several Coins, &c. 1736."

137. The Hue and Cry Of The Poor of Ireland For Small Change :
Or, Considerations on the many Inconveniences which our
People in general, as well as the Trade and Commerce of this
Kingdom labours under for Want of Brass or Copper-Coin.
As Also A proper Regulation in our Silver Specie. Humbly
offer'd to the Consideration of our State Physicians. By
Isaac Broadloom, Clothier.
> *Dublin : Printed in the Year* MDCCXXXI.
> *H.C.* 101.
> Rewritten from " The Drapier Reviv'd " the first part dwelling on
> the deficiency of Copper, whilst in the first pamphlet it was more
> general on scarcity of small money; therefore probably by Sir John
> Browne.

138. Proposals For Establishing of a Fund of 30000 l. to be vested
in a Corporation for the Purposes therein mentioned, Humbly
Submitted to the Consideration of all true Lovers of their
Country, particularly to the Right Honourable and Honourable the Lords Spiritual and Temporal and Commons, soon to
be assembled in Parliament.
> *Dublin : Printed by S. Powell, for the Author*, MDCCXXXI.
> 8vo. 27 pp. (Preface signed John Knightley).
> Scheme for a Lottery to raise money to further mining in Ireland,
> especially the coal mines in Ballycastle.

139. A Proposal Humbly offer'd to the P—T, for the more effectual
preventing the further Growth of Popery, &c.
> By D. S—t. To which is added, The Humble Petition of
> the Weavers and Venders of Gold and Silver Lace, Embroi-
> deries, &c.
> *Dublin Printed. London Re-printed for J. Roberts.*
> MDCCXXXI.
> 8vo. 32 pp.
> *U.C.—Hib.* 7. 731. 15.

140. Some Observations on The Present State Of Ireland, Particularly with Relation to the Woollen Manufacture. In a Letter
To his Excellency the Duke of Dorset.
> *Dublin : Printed in the Year* MDCCXXXI.
> Sm. 8vo. 24 pp.
> *H.C.* 101.
> H. and L. attribute this to Sir Richard Cox.
> Also a London edition same year, printed for Roberts. Probably
> the original.

141. Some Remarks On the Conduct of the Parliament of England,
As far as it relates to the Woollen Manufacture : With some
Animadversions on the Free Briton's Remarks on a Pamphlet,
entitled, Observations on the Present State of Ireland. By
the Author of the said Pamphlet.
> *London : T. Reynolds.* MDCCXXXI.
> 8vo. 32 pp. (at end) says Printed from the Dublin edition.
> (By Sir Richard Cox).
> *H.C.* 101.

142. The Interest And Trade Of Ireland Consider'd.

Dublin: Printed by Christopher Dickson, 1731: And Reprinted, 1732. With an Addition and a Letter for relieving the Poor distress'd Inhabitants of this Kingdom.

Sm. 8vo. 22 pp. Dedication signed Robert Wilson.

H.C.

Speaks of a great scarcity in 1709.

Suggests Granaries to be under the Control of the Linen Board. Also suggests a Duty of £20 a Tun on French wines; molasses to be admitted Duty-free. Also suggests lowering the duty on tobacco to prevent the smuggling which is now rife.

143. An Infallible Scheme To pay the Publick Debt Of This Nation In Six Months. Humbly offered to the Consideration of the present P - - - t. ....

Printed in the Year 1731.

12mo. 16 pp.

Another edition :—

An Infallible Scheme To pay the Publick Debt Of This Nation In Six Months. Humbly Offered to the Consideration of the present P - - - t. By D—n S—T. ....

Dublin, Printed. London, Reprinted for H. Whittridge. MDCCXXXII.

Sm. 8vo. 23 pp.

Roberts printed this in 1732 as part of "Schemes From Ireland For The Benefit of the Body Natural, Ecclesiastical and Politick."

This tract is sometimes ascribed to Swift, but is omitted by Sir Walter Scott and Temple Scott in their editions of his works.

144. A Letter To A Member of Parliament From A Country Gentleman, Concerning the Growth of the Wool, and the Nature of the Woollen Trade in Ireland; wherein such a Method is proposed for preventing the clandestine Exportation of those Commodities as will be equally beneficial to both Kingdoms.

Printed in the Year MDCCXXXII.

Sm. 8vo. 12 pp. Signed Hiberno Britannus.

Gall. L. 11. 92-10.

Another edition without date.

Favours linen industry against the woollen, and says the clandestine trade in wool should be stopped.

145. The Advantages Which may arise to the People of Ireland By raising of Flax and Flax-Seed, Considered. Together with Instructions for Sowing and Saving the Seed, and Preparing the Flax for the Market. Drawn up and Published by the Directions Of The Dublin Society. ....

Dublin: Printed by A. Rhames, Printer to the Dublin Society. MDCCXXXII.

8vo. 24 pp.

This is the first publication of this nature by the Society, which had been started in 1731 by Prior, Dr. Madden, and other public-spirited citizens.

A printed list of the members may be found in the Halliday Collection.

The Dublin Society still exists, and has the honour of being the oldest Institution of the kind in the Empire. During the 18th century it published a large number of tracts intended to promote Irish industries, but devoted itself chiefly to the improvement of Agriculture.

146. A Proposal For The Relief Of Ireland, By A Coinage Of Monies, of Gold, and Silver ; And establishing a National Bank.

London : Printed for J. Worrall, 1733.

Sm. 8vo. 29 pp.

H.C. 111.

This is by an unknown author, who may possibly be Bishop Berkeley.

This tract was reprinted in Dublin 1734 in 28 pp. with a 4 pp. preface, in which the author calls attention to the great difficulty which bankers encounter in Ireland in not being able to find saleable securities on which they could lend money.

The author also shows the absurdity of Prior's calculations about the loss by the Absentees. He wants a national coin so that the export of it could be prohibited. Refers to the attempt to start a bank in Ireland in 1697, and proposes a Bank of Credit based on land.

147. The Blessings of a Wooll-Trade : Or, The Irish Manufacturer's Plea, In A Letter From a Gentleman of the County, To A Merchant of the City of Cork.

Dublin : Printed and Sold by E. Waters. [*n. d.*]

Sm. 8vo. 13 pp. (Signed Hibernicus).

Gall. L. 11. 92-9.

This tract was also published in Cork with the same title, in 21 pp. 16mo.

As this letter is dated Bandon, Feb. 4th, 1732-40, it was probably written by Sir Richard Cox.

The author proposes an association to agree to purchase apparel or household furniture made only in Ireland.

148. The Draper's Remarks On the Late Importation Of New-Coin'd English Half-Pence, And the Consequences thereof to this Kingdom. With Modest Reasons for the Liberty of a Mint, &c. Humbly Offered to the Consideration of those at the Helm.

Dublin : Printed in the Year 1733.

Sm. 8vo. 8 pp.

Dix.

Probably 1773, but may be 1732, as part of the imprint is cut off.

Complains of an introduction of English Half-Pence, solely because this may interfere with the Irish obtaining a Mint of their own, a matter which was being greatly agitated at that time.

All the other objections offered would apply equally to coins made in Ireland.

Probably written by Sir John Browne, as it follows the lines of the "Drapier Revived," and other tracts of his in urging the establishment of an Irish Mint.

149. Ballycastle Collieries Set in their Proper Light : With Answer
To Several Observations Against The Benefit That may arise
to This Kingdom thereby.
Dublin : Faulkner. MDCCXXXIII.
H.C. 111.

150. Some Reasons Against the Bill for settling the Tyth of Hemp,
Flax, etc. by a Modus.
*Dublin : Printed by George Faulkner in Essex-Street,
opposite to the Bridge.* MDCCXXIV.
8vo.   20 pp.
(By Jonathan Swift).
The date is incorrect, should be 1734.

151. Some Useful Cautions To The Publick In A Letter To his
Grace &c. The Arch Bishop of Cashel.
Dublin Printed in the Year, 1734.
8vo.   8 pp.
H.C. 117.
Criticism of Browne's Letter to Cashel of 1731.

152. An Enquiry Into The Reasons Of The Decay Of Credit,
Trade, And Manufactures In Ireland.
Dublin : Printed for T. Moore. MDCCXXXV.
8vo.   36 pp.   Dedication signed Daniel Webb.
H.C. 121.
To reduce the Rate of Interest.
Wants Parliamentary notes at 3 per cent. Interest lent for 21
years to such as could give good security, equitably distributed over
the Kingdom to the amount of one million, and the interest to be
applied to educating poor Irish children in the Protestant religion.

153. A Letter To The Author of a Pamphlet, Entitled, An Enquiry
Into The Reasons Of The Decay Of Credit, Trade, And
Manufactures In Ireland.
By a Friend to the Author.
Dublin : Moore. MDCCXXXV.
8vo.   8 pp.
Dix.
Approves of Webb's idea of a Bank, but suggests that anyone that
receives these notes should pay down 10 per cent. in sterling, which
will act as a fund for circulating them.

154. An Appendix To A Pamphlet Entitled, An Enquiry Into The
Reasons Of The Decay Of Credit, Trade, And Manufactures
In Ireland.
Dublin : Moore. MDCCXXXV.
8vo.   30 pp.
(By Daniel Webb).
Dix.

155. Some Considerations On the Improvement of the Linen Manufacture, In Ireland, Particularly with Relation to the Raising and Dressing of Flax and Flax-Seed.
Dublin : Reilly, M,DCC,XXXV.
8vo. 40 pp.

156. The Querist, Containing Several Queries, Proposed to the Consideration Of The Public.
Dublin: Printed by R. Reilly, on Cork-Hill, For G. Risk, G. Ewing, and W. Smith, Booksellers in Dames-Street, M,DCC,XXV (*sic*).
8vo. 59 pp. 1 p. adv.
The same. Part II.
Dublin: Printed by R. Reilly on Cork Hill, For G. Risk, G. Ewing, and W. Smith, Booksellers in Dames-Street, M,DCC,XXXVI.
46 pp. 2 pp. adv.
The same. Part III.
Consult not with a Merchant concerning Exchange.
Ecclesiastes *c.* XXXVII. *v.* 11.
Dublin: Printed by R. Reilly on Cork-Hill, For Jos Leathley, Bookseller in Dames-Street. M,DCC,XXXVII.
60 pp.
(By George Berkeley).
The original edition of " The Querist." The date of Part I should be 1735 instead of 1725.

157. An Abstract Of The Number Of Protestant and Popish Families In the Several Counties and Provinces Of Ireland, Taken from the Returns made by the Hearthmoney Collectors, to the Hearthmoney Office in Dublin, in the Years 1732 and 1733. Those being reckon'd Protestant and Popish Families, where the Heads of Families are either Protestants or Papists. With Observations.
Dublin: Printed by M. Rhames, for R. Gunne, M.DCC.XXXVI.
8vo. 15 pp.
MS. note on title-page says by David Bindon. On p. 12 refers to Petty's " Political Survey of Ireland," published in 1672.
The observations of the author are of little importance, the chief interest lying in the figures themselves.
The only David Bindon that I can learn anything about apparently died in 1733, as his will was proven in that year in County Limerick. This naturally throws some doubt on his authorship of these observations.

158. A Letter From The Revd. J. S. D. S. P. D. To A Country Gentleman In The North of Ireland.
Printed in the Year, MDCCXXXVI.
8vo. 8 pp. Signed A. North.
H.C. 126.
In Massie's MS. Catalogue in the British Museum under date of

(46)

1736, appears "A Letter to a Country Gentleman about Coin in Ireland," and ascribed to Swift. This entry no doubt is intended to indicate this tract.

No. 19 of The Intelligencer, which is undoubtedly by Swift, relates to this same subject, and is also signed A. North. I suspect this tract therefore to be a reprint from the Intelligencer; unfortunately I have not both at hand to compare them.

159. A Letter From A Gentleman In The North of Ireland, To His Friend in Dublin, In Relation to the Regulation of the Coin.
   Dublin: Printed in the Year MDCCXXXVI.
   8vo. 8 pp.
   H.C. 126.
   Speaks of the great scarcity of small gold and silver in the North, most of the gold being foreign £4 pieces, which have to be weighed.
   On this account a new set of Coiners have started up, who coin copper penny and twopenny tickets not worth one-tenth of what they pass for, under the denomination of a note. "I promise to pay the Bearer on Demand two Pence:" Signed A.B. Many hundreds of pounds are already out and increasing, and everybody is forced to accept them. One must pay 6d. in the pound to get £4 gold changed to small gold, and then 6d. more to get the small gold changed to silver.

160. An Answer To The Remonstrances Of The People of Ireland, Against making any Alteration in the Coin.
   By their Friends in Great Britain; Containing Reasons for Regulating the Coin, with regard to the Trade between the two Kingdoms.
   London: Printed, and Dublin Re-printed, MDCCXXXVI.
   8vo. 8 pp.
   B.M. 8227. aaa. 23.
   The writer objects to Ireland raising the value of British Coin in Ireland, and speaks of a Proclamation to be issued in London the next day to regulate the British Coin.

161. Some Considerations On Lowering the Gold.
   (at end) *Dublin: Printed at the Rein Deer in Montrath-Street*, 1736. [*Dated April* 20 *and signed J——*].
   2 folio sheets.
   H.C. 126.
   * In the volume in which this occurs this part of the tract is bound in and the signature cannot be read.

162. Remarks Upon A Paper Just Publish'd Intitl'd Some Considerations On Lowering the Gold.
   Dublin: Printed in the Year MDCCXXXVI.
   8vo. 16 pp.
   H.C. 126.
   Says silver is the measure and not gold.

163. Reasons Why We should not Lower the Coins Now Current in this Kingdom, Occasion'd by a Paper, intitled, Remarks on the Coins Current in this Kingdom.
Dublin : Faulkner, 1736.
Sm. 8vo.   15 pp.
B.M. 104, *K.* 32.

Another edition.
Reasons Why we should not Lower the Coins Now current in this Kingdom.   Occasioned by a Paper Intituled, Remarks on the Coins current in this Kingdom.   To which is added, The Rev. Dean Swift's Opinion, Delivered by him, in an Assembly of above One hundred and Fifty eminent Merchants who met at the Guild Hall, on Saturday the 24th of April, 1736, in order to draw up their Petition, and Present it to his Grace the Lord-Lieutenant against lowering said Coin.
Dublin : Printed and sold by E. Waters.
Sm. 8vo.   8 pp.
B.M. 8225, *aa.* 7.

Proposes raising the silver instead of lowering the gold.   Attributes the loss of silver largely to the smugglers, who lie off the Coasts, and retail perishable goods, for which the country runs to them and carries the change.

Wants to raise the small silver coins above their intrinsic value, so that it will not pay to export them.

164. Some Observations On The Present Currency, As well as the Intrinsick Value Of the Several Coins In This Kingdom.   In a Letter to A. S. Esq;
Dublin : Printed in the Year 1736.
Sm. 8vo.   16 pp.
H.C.

The writer says he shipped to Rotterdam ducats weighing 20 dwts. and 16 grains, and cobbs weighing 17 dwts.   Ducats pass at 6s. and cobbs at 4s. 9d. (pieces of eight), 3 half-pence off for each half-penny-weight wanting.

The ducats brought 3 guilders 3 stivers, and occasionally 3 guilders 5 stivers, depending on the East Indian demand.   Common Exchange rate is 24½d. Irish for a guilder.   So he got 6s. 5d. for each ducat.— Cobbs brought 50-52 stivers, and after remittance 5s. 1¼d. and 5s. 3½d.

Several hundred cobbs lately brought from Spain were bought for exportation to England at 5s. 10d. per oz., which he says is the real value of sterling in Ireland.   So the pieces cost 5s. and ½d. each and weighed slightly over 17 dwts. each ; therefore, why should these cobbs pass at 4s. 9d., when by taking them to Skinners Row they will bring 5s.   Even merchants sometimes pay more than 5s. 10d. per oz. for sterling silver.

Exchange rules 2-4 per cent., sometimes 5-6 per cent. above the real difference in the currency of the money in England and Ireland.

Advocates raising the silver coin to its bullion value, namely 5s. 10d. per oz. ; to lower the gold is to begin at the wrong end.

Thinks the practice of weighing current coins a loss and obstacle to trade, but there is no reason to weigh French, Spanish and Portuguese, and not those of England.

The larger the piece of gold the more it is over-valued, owing apparently to not weighing to half grains.

Asserts that English silver is so scarce, that the linen manufacturers have to give a premium of 3d. to 6d. per pound for it.

The regulations should be 5s. 10d. per oz. for silver, and 86s. 8d. per oz. for gold, or 4s. 4d. per dwt., no matter where it comes from.

As bullion is a commodity we purchase with our goods, we ought to fix such a price on it so to be able to export it without loss, in case any redundancy falls into our hands; too much money being an insupportable evil.

I have given large extracts from this because many details are given of actual transactions, which show better the actual value of the coins current at the time than any of the Cambists or Negociators of the day.

As the tract is nothing but an amplification of no. 139, it is certainly by the same author, probably Sir John Browne.

165. A Proposal For Giving Badges To The Beggars In All The Parishes of Dublin.
　　By the Dean of St. Patricks.
　　Dublin: MDCCXXXVII.
　　H.C. 134.

The original edition was printed in London the same year in small quarto by T. Cooper.

166. Woods upon Woods; Or A Bigger Trap Newly Laid, To Ensnare the People of Ireland. For Brass-Money Is Now Hibernia's Portion Instead of Her Sterling Treasure.
　　Dublin: Waters, 1737.
　　12mo. 8 pp., signed James Maculla.
　　H.C. 135.

167. A Short Answer to Short Reasons Why Our Gold-Money in Ireland Should not be Lower'd.
　　Dublin: Printed in the Year 1737.
　　8vo. 8 pp.
　　H.C. 135.

168. A Reply To The Principal Arguments For The Reduction of the Gold Coin, And some Considerations on the Causes thereof. Dedicated to the Right Honourable Sir Richard Cox, Baronet.
　　Dublin: Rider, 1737.
　　8vo. 56 pp.
　　H.C. 135.

169. A Letter To A Member of Parliament, Concerning the Late Reduction Of The Gold-Coin.
　　Dublin: Printed in the Year M,DCC,XXXVII.
　　8vo. 28 pp. [MS. note by Ed. Bruce].
　　H.C.

Old arguments about the $2\frac{1}{2}$ per cent. saved on remittances to absentees by using Portugal gold over-valued.

On account of the reduction, Exchange fell from 11 per cent. to $8\frac{1}{3}$ per cent.

Refutes clearly the idea that there had been any loss on exports by over-valuing the gold.

Effect of the reduction was to raise rents 3 per cent., as the value of goods (export, at least) cannot be raised 3 per cent.

According to this writer the par of exchange is not 107¾.

Forgets to mention that as all prices will eventually be reduced by 3¼ per cent., there will be no losers except the people who have the actual coins and debtors who contracted in the old currency. Argues from standpoint of manufacturer or merchant, who sees the difficulty of lowering costs of production and inability to raise prices abroad.

Says the whole evil was scarcity of small gold and silver.

Proposes a new Irish silver coinage to be made, a small matter less intrinsically valuable than gold.

Also suggests a law to reduce all contracts 10 per cent., and give all money in Ireland the same currency as in England.

170. Some Reflections Upon the Present Regulation of the Coin : Offer'd to the Consideration of the Poor of Ireland.
    n.d. n.p. (but Dublin, 1737).
    1 folio sheet.

171. Queries Relating to the New Half-Pence, and lowering the Coin. Address'd to all the good People of Ireland.
    Printed in the Year 1737.
    4to. 10 pp.
    B.M. 8828, *e.* 23.
    Objects largely on constitutional grounds, as having been done without consent or advice of Parliament.

Q. 15. Whether the bankers have not basely sacrificed the interest and welfare of the country to the most lucrative and sordid motives, also (17) whether the banker has not power to ruin numbers of people.

Whether £30,000 of Portugal gold was not exported within 3 days after the proclamation ; and whether 5 times as much has not been sent away since. Thinks it was sent to London and sold by the ounce, and that the alteration has multiplied delays in trade. Thinks it would have been better to have raised the silver.

Suggests reducing civil and military list by 3¾ per cent.

In Q. 33 refers to a noted banker as Strap behind the Coach, and says he was only worth £100 in 1703 ; he is a noted jobber in gold and silver coins, and has exported large quantities of both since August 1st, and lent money at 6 per cent. to import the copper half-pence, and suggests Parliament addressing the King to remove him from all places of honour and trust.

35 Queries in all.

172. An Unprejudic'd Enquiry Into The Nature and Consequences Of The Reduction Of Our Gold.
    Dublin : Printed in the Year MDCCXXXVII.
    8vo. 15 pp.

173. The Parliament And Corporations of Ireland's Declaration, and Protest Against Foreign Brass-Money. Set forth in a Supplement to Woods upon Woods ; Or, Hibernia in a Wood, About taking Britannia's Counterfeit Half-Pence and Farthings......
    Dublin : Printed in the Year MDCCXXXVII.
    12mo. 15 pp., signed James Maculla.
    H.C. 135.

174. A Short Essay On Coin.
  Dublin: Printed in the Year 1737.
  8vo. 22 pp.
  (By Bryan Robinson).

  Contains the three representations of Sir Isaac Newton dated respectively March 3, 1712, June 23, 1712, and Sept. 21, 1717.
  This was afterwards expanded into a much larger work and published in 1757.
  Also gives some arithmetical formulas for comparing values of different coins.

175. An Appendix To a Short Essay On Coin.
  Dublin: Printed in the Year 1737.
  8vo. 8 pp.
  (By Bryan Robinson).
  H.C. 135.

176. Two and Two make Four : In A Letter To The Honest Traders Of Ireland.
  Dublin: Printed in the Year MDCCXXXVII.
  8vo. 8 pp.
  H.C. 135.

177. Some Reflections, Concerning the Reduction of Gold Coin in Ireland. Upon the Principle of the Dean of St. Patrick's and Mr. Lock : Humbly submitted to the Good People of Ireland.
  Dublin: Printed in the Year M,DCC,XXXVII.
  8vo. 16 pp.
  T.C.D.—R. R. 11, 26, *no.* 12.
  Recalls Swift's Remarks in the Intelligencer, No. 19.

178. The Lord Knows What, By the Lord knows Who.
  (at end) *Meath-Street Printed: By the Lord knows who,* 1737.
  1 folio sheet.

  Various references to the Primate, Dean Swift and others. Opposes the reduction of the gold coin, which had just taken place.

179. A Letter from a Gentleman in the Country to his Friend in Dublin.

  Quoted in a Letter to a Member of Parliament concerning the late reduction of the gold coin.

180. A Compleat System Of The Revenue of Ireland, In its several Branches of Import, Export, and Inland Duties.
  Dublin: Reilly, M,DCC,XXXVII.
  8vo, xiv (4), 456-79 App.
  By Thomas Bacon.

181. A Brief Enquiry Into The Nature and Use Of Premiums,
With Respect to Trade.
Dublin : Printed in the Year M,DCC,XXXVII.
8vo. 42 pp.

Very lucid explanation of the effect of bounties on exportation or
importation, with incidental criticism of the bounty on the export of
wheat in England. Advocates for Ireland, premiums on new processes
and improved product, importing a better class of seeds and dis-
tributing same gratis ; hiring agricultural experts, erection of granaries,
etc. The plan somewhat following the lines of the Linen Boards.

182. An Argument Upon The Woollen Manufacture Of Great
Britain. Plainly demonstrating, That Ireland must be
speedily employed therein, as the only means to recover its
Decay, and to prevent its Ruin. ......
Dublin : Faulkner, MDCCXXXVII. (published first in March
1735). (in London ?).
sm. 8vo. 26 pp.
B.M. 8245. *aa.* 6.

The Interests of England, as they are now understood, are the
Interests of Particulars against the Public.
Claims the abolition of the Woollen Manufacture has drawn 20,000
people from the country to foreign countries, and brought about the
consequent establishment of the Manufacture in almost all parts of
Europe.
Pleads for permission for Ireland to re-engage in the Woollen Manu-
facture, on the basis of justice and also expediency, as the only man-
ner of combating the French manufactures, which easily undersell the
English.
Post. 24 to end is Criticism of the Golden Fleece.

183. Agriculture The surest Means of National Wealth : And An
Impartial Administration Of Justice The best Encouragement to
National Industry. Together with several Improvements in
Agriculture recommended ; but especially the Propagation of
Saint Foin, and La Lucerne. ....
Dublin : Reilly, MDCCXXXVIII.
8vo. 31 pp.

184. Reflections And Resolutions Proper For The Gentlemen of
Ireland, As to their Conduct for the Service of their Country,

As Landlords,	As Country Gentlemen and Farmers,
As Masters of Families,	As Justices of the Peace,
As Protestants,	As Merchants,
As descended from British Ancestors,	As Members of Parliament.

......
Dublin : Reilly, MDCCXXXVIII.
8vo. 237 pp.
(By Samuel Madden).
B.M. 601. *g.* 15.
Republished in Dublin 1816.

185. A Swift Warning To The People Of Ireland, Collected From The King and Parliament and Magistrates of this Kingdom's Grant to Prevent the Crown and Revenue, and Nation being wrong'd and losing a Hundred Thousand Pounds per Annum.
Dublin: Rider. 1738.
8vo. 16 pp.
(By James Maculla).
H.C. 137.

On the adulteration of brass and pewter by the manufacturers of Ireland. Recites a grant by the Pewterers of England and Corporation of London to James Maculla of the several tin, plate and lay metal Standards, that he may put into effect the law of Jan. 1st, 1697, which provided that the pewter and brass of Ireland should be of same quality as that required in London. This in 1710 and confirmed in Dublin in various years afterwards.

Recites attempts to evade the law.

186. Some Thoughts On The Tillage of Ireland : Humbly Dedicated To the Parliament. ...
To which is Prefixed, A Letter to the Printer, from the Reverend Doctor Swift, Dean of St. Patrick's, recommending the following Treatise.
Dublin: Faulkner. M,DCC,XXXVIII.
8vo. Tit. 2 Swift's Letter. 54 pp.
H.C. 137.

Probably by Arthur Dobbs, as it is an exemplification of the facts and argument set forth on pp. 22-23 in Part I of his Essay on the Trade of Ireland, 1729. This demonstration is further referred to as Dobbs' in the " Dialogue between Dean Swift & Tho. Prior " 1753.

The argument is to prove the greater profit to the nation from Tillage than from Grazing, although Dobbs acknowledges the profit to the individual raiser is greater from grazing.

Lecky gives this as printed in London in 1737.

3rd Edition by same, 1741.

187. Four Letters Originally written in French, Relating to the Kingdom of Ireland, Accompanied with Remarks. To which is added, A fifth Letter by the same Author, containing a Computation of the Number of Inhabitants in all the Kingdoms and chief Cities of Europe, with a Conjecture concerning the Number of all the People that have lived upon the Face of the Earth, from the Creation to the present Time.
Dublin. Reilly. MDCCXXXIX.
sm. 8vo. 34 pp.
H.C. 144.

Letters dated 1735.

188. A Letter To Every Well-Wisher Of Trade and Navigation. Containing A Relation of the Author's Discoveries in the Nymph-Fishing-Bank, &c. &c. Remarks on the Dutch and other Foreign Fisheries : And Means proposed for Rendering our Own successful. Most humbly Inscribed to the Legislature of Ireland. By William Doyle, Hydrographer.
Dublin: Reilly. M,DCC,XXXIX.
8vo. Tit. Map and 20 pp.
H.C. 144.

189. A Letter To The Dublin-Society, On The Improving Their
Fund ; And The Manufactures, Tillage, etc. In Ireland. ......
Dublin : Printed by R. Reilly. M,DCC,XXXIX.
This Pamphlet is printed on Irish Paper, made by Mr.
Randal, at Newbridge near Leixlip.
8vo. 56 pp.
(By Samuel Madden).
H.C. 144.

190. A Letter From A Gentleman In The Country, To A Member
Of Parliament.
Dublin : Faulkner, MDCCXXXIX.
sm. 8vo. 13 pp. (Dated 30th Oct. 1739.)
U.C. Hib. 7. 739. (7).

On the neglect of mining. Speaks of a few mines of copper, lead
and coal already opened, but very few and not well worked. Therefore
suggests public support. Also refining and smelting houses should
be erected at public expense. Suggests a Society with an Annual
Fund, similar to Linen Society, to encourage this work.

191. Some Considerations On The Laws Which Incapacitate
Papists From Purchasing Lands, From Taking long or beneficial Leases, And From Lending Money on real Securities.
Dublin : Faulkner, MDCCXXXIX.
8vo. 39 pp.

An economic treatment of the question.
In this he asserts that the law which regulated the descent of real
property belonging to Papists (in Gavelkind) had brought more Papists
over than anything else and had less of persecution in it. Asserts
there are not over 20 Papists in Ireland possessing £1000 yearly in
Lands. The Papists have however engrossed a great share of the Trade
and Commerce.

192. Some Thoughts On The Importance Of The Linnen-Manufacture
To Ireland, And How To Lessen the Expence of it.
Dublin : Faulkner. MDCCXXXIX.
8vo. 26 pp.
H.C. 148.

Chiefly a technical essay on the process of preparing flax.

193. A Collection Of Papers, Relating to a Scheme, laid before the
Trustees of the Linen Manufacture, For The More Effectual
Reformation Of Lappers. By Robert Ross, Junior, Esq.
Dublin : Reilly. MDCCXXXIX.
8vo. xviii. 58 pp.
H.C. 144.

Lappers were Public Inspectors appointed, who after passing linen,
affixed a stamp, showing quality.
The writer accuses Lappers of fraud and carelessness and for this
reason favours abolishing them.

194. The Case Of John Hay, And the other separate Creditors of Samuel Burton, Esq; deceased.

Humbly offered to the Consideration of the Creditors of the Bank lately kept by the said Samuel Burton and Daniel Falkiner, Esqs.

Dublin: Printed in the Year MDCCXL.

8vo. 42 pp.

H.C. 151.

The Bank stopped Jan. 25th, 1733. The tract contains many particulars of the settlement.

195. The Case Of Oswald Edwards, Being An Impartial and faithful Account of the several and great Services he has done for the Creditors of the Bank lately kept by Samuel Burton and Daniel Falkiner, Esqrs. And of the ill-natured and ungenerous Treatment which he has had from Robert Roberts, Esq.

Dublin: Powell. MDCCXL.

8vo. 77 pp.

H.C. 151.

This pamphlet contains many particulars about the winding up of the affairs of this Bank. From this the Creditors had up to this received 15s. in the pound, and would receive more.

196. Considerations On The Present Calamities Of This Kingdom ; And The Causes of the Decay Of Public Credit With The Means of Restoring It.

Dublin: Printed and sold by the Booksellers. MDCCXL.

sm. 8vo. 17 pp.

U.C. Hib. 7. 749. 13.

The unrestrained system of private Banking was due to a belief, that no other could be equally capable of contributing that Assistance to Trade, held to be necessary for its subsistence, from a Paper substitute for Money. Bankers largely lend their Credit on Mortgage of Estates (except Finlay & Co., which in effect has been a Discount Office). Some Bankers issued notes in excess of their Deposits, and thus made large Profits ; but the Securities were slow of realization, and six Banks had broken in 5 years past from this cause, for a total of little less than one million.

Effect of too much paper, is to restrict Exports and stimulate Imports, thus creating a drain of specie. This reduced the amount ot specie available to meet the excessive issues of notes.

Since the failures of Banks, circulating of paper is greatly restricted, and there is a noticeable improvement in Exports of Linen, while Imports have lessened in the last two years.

Proposes restricting Banking to Persons of at least £40,000 real or personal Estate, and prohibiting lending on Mortgages or other Securities not convertible within six months. Not to be permitted to loan more than twice the amount of capital, nor follow any other trade, and that Bankers on one or two days in the year be obliged to render a statement, including that of the Nature and Amount of their Securities.

197. The Distress'd State Of Ireland Considered ; More Particularly With Respect to the North. In a Letter to a Friend.

Printed in the Year M,DCC,XL.

8vo. 52 pp.

H.C. 151.

About bad harvests and scarcity, &c. from 1728 to 1740. High prices and several losses of the Potato Crop. This year also is a very severe one, many farmers being obliged to buy bread.

Still the Rents keep rising.

Quotes " Present miserable state of Ireland," which had probably been recently reprinted, as he says it was written about three years ago.

Largely devoted to an attack on tythes, and gives an interesting account of the economic state of Ireland.

The severe frost began about Christmas, 1739.

198. A Letter From A Country Gentleman In The Province of Munster, To his Grace the Lord Primate Of All Ireland.

8vo. 8 pp. (no regular title, if published) dated Cashel May 25th, 1741. (Signed Publicola).

H.C. 161.

Calls for a Tillage Act, asserting that the famine is due to want of corn, due to the grass pastures of the large land-owners, and advocates a system of public granaries, which had been put forward by Arthur Dobbs.

Given by Lecky as printed in Dublin in 1741.

Halliday's copy without regular title as well.

See 199 for author.

199. A Dissertation On The Inlargement Of Tillage, The Erecting of Public Granaries, and The Regulating, Employing, and Supporting the Poor in this Kingdom : Addressed to his Grace the Lord Primate of all Ireland.

Dublin : Powell. MDCCXLI.

8vo. 70 pp. (Signed Publicola).

H.C. 161.

An amplification of the views expressed in the preceding letter.

The Lough Fea Library Catalogue gives this tract as by Thomas Dawson, LL.B. If true, it fixes the identity of "Publicola," who wrote several interesting tracts about this time and later.

200. The Necessity Of Tillage and Granaries. In A Letter To A Member of Parliament Living in the County of — ....

Dublin : Printed in the Year M,DCC,XLI.

8vo. 64 pp. (Signed Triptolemus).

H.C. 161.

According to Bradshaw copy in U.C. this tract is by P. Skelton.

201. A Proposal For Lessening the Excessive Price Of Bread Corn In Ireland. ......

Dublin : Reilly, M,DCC,XLI.

Sm. 8vo. 36 pp.

B.M. 8245. *aa.* 7.

A 3rd edition in 1757. Printed by S. Powell, 36 pp.

H.C. 277.

Speaks of extreme winter of 1739 followed by backward spring and scarcely any summer. This brought on a famine and general sickness, that nearly depopulated some parts of the country.

Suggests more and better tillage and Granaries.

Here suggests one if not the real chief reason of the small tillage of

Wheat, and that was that the May rents must be paid before Winter, and the easiest way to do it was to raise Barley and ship the same early, largely to Portugal, while Wheat could not be ready. And yet he asserts the raising of Wheat is 25 per cent. more profitable than Barley.

Also asserts that a bill for giving a Premium on Exportation of corn came over from England in 1710, approved of by the Queen and Council of England, but was thrown out in the Irish House.

202. A Proposal For Erecting Granaries In The City Of Dublin, And other Parts of the Kingdom, To prevent any Scarcity Of Corn For The Future.
   Dublin : Reilly, M,DCC,XLI.
   8vo.   8 pp.
   (By Thomas Prior).
   H.C. 160.

Suggests two in Dublin and one in each of the principal cities. A Fund to be subscribed by persons, formed into Companies by Act of Parliament, to fill the same.   To fix a maximum price of 23/- per bushel of 20 stone from April 1 to Sept. 1, and shall be obliged to buy at 12/-.   When price over 18/- not to buy in Ireland, nor sell at all in Ireland while price under 15/-.

To store 40,000 bushels in Dublin and smaller quantities elsewhere. Also suggests a Govt. guarantee of 4 per cent. on stock subscribed.

The author's name is on the reprint, entitled "A Proposal to prevent the Price of Corn from Rising too high," etc.—n. d. n. p.

203. The Groans Of Ireland.   In A Letter To A Member Of Parliament.   —
   Dublin : Faulkner, M,DCC,XLI.
   8vo.   28 pp.
   B.M. 8145. *b.* 54.

Extremely interesting and valuable tract, as first proposing to issue notes against deposits of corn in public granaries, the circulation to be guaranteed, and their convertibility as well, by Corn Banks to be erected, which should receive from the granaries 3 per cent. on the amount of the Bills so guaranteed.   The Bank to be formed by paying in 20 per cent. in cash of the capital, which he considered sufficient to ensure convertibility.   A Price to be paid for corn to be fixed, and no corn allowed to be exported except by the granaries, which might sell at the best price they could get abroad, but were to be restricted to selling at home to 1/- per bushel over the agreed price.

In effect a scheme for an elastic currency.

204. Scarcity of Bread No Private Conspiracy Or, Combination : Or, The Draper inform'd of the True Cause.
   Dublin : Powell, MDCCXLI.
   8vo.   15 pp.
   H.C. 161.

Complains of the difficulty of collecting tythes, and attributes the scarcity of wheat to the preference of farmers for grazing instead of tillage, part of which he attributes to the tythe system, or rather to the dislike of it, and attempts to evade it.

205. A Scheme For Utterly Abolishing The present Heavy and
Vexatious Tax of Tithe. In A Letter To a Member of
Parliament.
Dublin: G. Ewing. M,DCC,XLII.
8vo. 14 pp. + 1.
H.C. 163.

206. The Farmer's Letters To The Protestants Of Ireland. [6 in
all of 8 pp. each].
Dublin: Faulkner. MDCCXLV.
H.C. 186.
Chiefly on the Dangers from France, Spain and the Church
of Rome.
(By Henry Brooke).
Reprinted in 1746 *as* "The Farmers Six Letters, etc."
B.M. T. 1623(8).

Chas. Kingsley wrote a biographical preface to Brooke's "Fool of
Quality" for an edition in 1859, and E. H. Baker has written a new
life of Brooke to another edition in 1906, which also contains Kingsley's sketch.
Brooke was one of the literary lights of Dublin in the middle of the
18th century, and was the author of many works, but is now chiefly
remembered for his "Fool of Quality."

207. Remarks On The Present State Of The Linnen-Manufacture
Of This Kingdom. Queries Relating To The Further Im-
provement thereof. Humbly Address'd to the Right Honble
Henry Boyle, Esq; Speaker to the Commons of Ireland.
Dublin: Faulkner. MDCCXLV.
8vo. 19 pp.
H.C. 188.

208. A Letter To A Member of Parliament, Concerning A Bankruptcy Bill.
Dublin: Esdall. M,DCC,XLV.
8vo. 8 pp.
U.C. Hib. 7. 745. 15.

209. A List Of The Absentees Of Ireland, And The Yearly Value
Of Their Estates and Incomes Spent Abroad. With Observations on the present Trade and Condition of that Kingdom.
By Thomas Prior, Esq.; The Third Edition; with Additions. ...
Dublin: Gunne, MDCCXLV.
8vo. Tit. 8 pp. Ded. and Preface. 94 pp. + 1 Table of Commodities, imported into Ireland for 3 years ending March 25,
1743.

With exception of a fresh address to the Reader, a Letter dated
Nov. 8, 1745, on the Rebellion, and the List inserted on a sheet, this
appears to be a reprint of the 2nd edition with the above additions.

210. A Draught Of The Heads of a Bill To Prevent Frauds Committed By Bankrupts, &c. Prepared By the Merchants and Traders of the City of Dublin, And By Them intended to be laid before the Legislative Power of this Kingdom, the next Session of Parliament.
Dublin: Reilly. MDCCXLV.
8vo. 58 pp.
H.C. 188.

211. An Account Of The Nature and Condition Of A Charter, To be granted for the working and manufacturing Mines and Minerals in Ireland; Together with Some general Heads relating to the Advantages that must necessarily result from that laudable Establishment.
In A Letter to the Right Honourable Thomas Lord Southwell. By Mr. O'Connor.
London: Printed in the Year 1745.
8vo. 8 pp.
H.C. 184.
States that he has been soliciting a Royal Charter for past five years. This gives plan of the Company.

212. Thoughts Of Present Concernment, For the Relief of the Poor In a Scarcity of Corn. Shewing Some experienced Methods new and old, whereby a poor Man is enabled, on poor Ground, to Garden, and thereby with small Expence of either Time, Labour or Money, make a comfortable and speedy Provision for his Family in either a scarce or plentiful Year. Designed at first as Part of the Employment, and for raising Part of the Subsistence of Boys educated in Charter-Schools, especially those founded on poor shallow Grounds, and now published for the Benefit of the Poor in general, against the Scarcity of the coming Summer.
By a Member of the Incorporated Society.
Dublin: Powell, MDCCXLVI.
8vo. 16 pp.
(By David Stephens).

213. Some Reasons Humbly offered, for Supporting and Continuing The Dublin Market For Linen-Yarn, As it is now Settled and Established in the Yarn-Hall, Lately erected near the Linen-Hall.
Dublin: Printed in the Year MDCCXLVII.
8vo. 20 pp.
H.C. 209.

214. Letters On Trade. Letter I. To the Farmer. ....
Dublin: Printed by Halhed Garland. M.DCC.XLVIII.
8vo. 8 pp.
also,

A Second Letter On Trade. To the Farmer. ....
Dublin : Printed by Halhed Garland. M.DCC.XLVIII.
8vo. 16 pp.

I believe these two Letters to have been written by James Digges La Touche. La Touche certainly wrote two Letters on Trade, and these are the only Letters that I have ever seen with that Title. Furthermore, the Second Letter is rather a remarkable production, and quite worthy of one of the leading merchants of the day in Dublin. It is chiefly devoted to a discussion of the function of money and the true significance of foreign trade. His explanations are more in accordance with our present ideas upon these subjects, than those which were current in the middle of the 18th century.

215. An Essay Towards An Historical Account Of Irish Coins, And Of The Currency of Foreign Monies In Ireland. With An Appendix : Containing Several Statutes, Proclamations, Patents, Acts of State, and Letters relating to the Same. ......

By James Simon, of Dublin, Merchant, F.R.S.
Dublin : Printed by S. Powell, For the Author, MDCCXLIX,
4to. xv + 184 pp. 8 Plates Coins.

216. A Letter From Sir Richard Cox, Bart. To Thomas Prior, Esq; Shewing from Experience, A sure Method to establish the Linen-Manufacture, and the Beneficial Effects it will immediately produce. ......
Dublin : Wilson. MDCCXLIX.
8vo. 48 pp.
The Third Edition. To which is added, An Appendix, containing a further Account of the Increase of the Linen Manufacture, to the Years 1749 and 1750.
Dublin : Wilson. MDCCLII. 44 pp.
H.C. 221.
Also London, reprinted, and same, 2nd edition in 1749.

Most interesting account of Cox's establishing the linen-manufacture on his Estate in Ireland, a domestic Industry among his Tenants, encouraged by a system of premiums, etc.

217. A Letter From Sir Richard Cox, Bart. To The High-Sheriff of the County of Cork. Relative to the present State of the Linen-Manufacture in that County ; And Further Means of Improving it.
Dublin : Peter Wilson. MDCCLIX.
8vo. 43 pp.
H.C. 221.

218. A Proposal For the better preventing Frauds In The Collection of the Customs Of The City of Dublin. Offered in the Year 1742. By Martin Kirkpatrick, Citizen and Goldsmith. With A Preface.
Dublin : James. 1749.
H.C. 221.

219. A Vindication Of The Broad Cloth Weavers. Being, The
Journeymens Answer To Mr. Textor's Letter In The Six-
teenth Censor. Number II.
Dublin: Sheppard. MDCCXLIX.
8vo. 7 pp.
H.C. 221.

220. Dean Swift's Ghost, To The Citizens of Dublin. Concluding
with a Word particularly to the Weavers.
Dublin: Printed in the Year 1749.
8vo. 8 pp.
H.C. 221.

221. The Case Of The Silk and Worsted Weavers In A Letter To
A Member of Parliament.
Dublin: Printed in the Year 1749.
8vo. 8 pp.
H.C. 221.
About apprentices; journeymen desiring to restrict their number.

222. An Appeal To The People of Ireland. Occasioned by the
Insinuations and Misrepresentations of the Author of a
Weekly Paper, Entitled, The Censor. Proving, that the
Principles laid down in that Paper, and the Author's Reflec-
tions upon England, are unjust, ungrateful, and in their
Consequence, highly injurious to the Linen Manufacture, to
the Charter Schools, and to the whole Protestant Interest of
Ireland.
By a Member of the Incorporated Society for promoting
English Protestant Schools in Ireland. The Second Edition.
Dublin: Wilson. MDCCXLIX.
8vo. 15 pp.
H.C. 221.

223. An Essay To Encourage And Extend The Linen-Manufacture
In Ireland, By Praemiums and other Means. By Thomas
Prior, Esq;
Dublin, Faulkner, MDCCXLIX.
8vo. 58 pp.
B.M. 8145. *c.* 10.
2nd edition, same except with Postscript (58 pp.)
B.M. 117. *h.* 55.
Postscript alludes to Sir Richard Cox's Tract.

224. A Letter From Hugh Boyd, Esq; Of Ballycastle To A Member
of Parliament, On the Late Scarcity of Coals In The City of
Dublin.
Dublin: Printed in the Year 1749-50.
8vo. 12 pp.
H.C. 221.

225. The Querist, Containing Several Queries, Proposed to the Consideration Of The Public. By the Bishop of Cloyne. .... Second Edition with Additions.
Dublin : Faulkner, MDCCL.
8vo. 67 pp.
Fourth and Fifth Editions, same year, by Faulkner.
Also London Edition same, "To which is added, by the same Author, A Word to the Wife : Or, An Exhortation to the Roman Catholic Clergy of Ireland." *Printed for W. Innys and others*, 1750, in 83 pp. 8vo.

These editions differ considerably from the original, there being now 595 Queries ; besides, a number that appeared in the first edition have been omitted, the subjects that they discussed having lost their importance.

226. Plan Of The Universal Register Office Now Open'd Opposite to the Parliament-House in College-Green.
Dublin : Powell, 1750.
8vo. 16 pp.
H.C. 233.

227. A Representation Of The State Of The Trade of Ireland, Laid before the House of Lords of England, On Tuesday the 10th of April, 1750, On Occasion of a Bill before that House, for laying a Duty on Irish Sail Cloth imported into Great-Britain.
Dublin : James Esdall, 1750.
8vo. 28 pp.
H.C. 233.
MS. on Title "by the Rt. Honble Earl of Egmont."
2nd edition by Faulkner—1750. 28 pp.

228. A Letter To A Member of Parliament, Complaining Of some Public Grievances, relating to the Kingdom in general, and this City in particular. With Proper Schemes for redressing them.
By a Lover of his Country.
Dublin : Printed for the Author, 1750.
8vo. 16 pp. Signed Richard Poekrich.
H.C. 233.

229. Some Considerations On The British Fisheries. With a Proposal For Establishing A General Fishery On The Coasts of Ireland. Addressed to the Rt. Honourable the Lord —
Dublin : Wilson, 1750.
8vo. 15 pp.
H.C. 229.

230. A Conversation Between a Blacksmith And A Merchant, Upon The Subject of passing Guineas by Weight only.

Dublin : Printed in the Year MDCCL.

8vo. 8 pp.

H.C. 233.

Favours this on account of the great amount of clipped and light weight gold in currency, or else recommends a recoinage. Some guineas short 3 to 5 shillings. Filing going on everywhere.

231. A Proposal For Uniting the Kingdoms Of Great Britain And Ireland.

London, Printed : And Dublin, Re-printed, Richard James, M,DCC,LI.

8vo. 46 pp.

232. An Answer To the Late Proposal For Uniting the Kingdom Of Great Britain and Ireland ; In some Occasional Remarks upon the Proposal itself.

Dublin. Exshaw. M,DCC,LI.

8vo. 48 pp.

U.C.—Hib. 7. 750. 4 (8).

Largely on the Trade of Ireland.

233. A State Of The Case Of The Creditors Of Burton's Bank. In which is Contained, A Narrative of the Proceedings Relative to the Demands of the said Creditors, against the Estate of Francis Harrison, Esq; deceased. Together With A Collection of the Papers Published, both for and against the Proposal, lately made by Abraham Creichton, Esq; to the said Creditors.

Dublin : Printed in the Year M,DCC,LI.

8vo. 53 pp. (Contains also a Reprint of the various letters published in this case in 1751).

H.C.

Bank stopped in 1733, and gives a history of the case of Samuel Burton and Daniel Falkiner.

The deficiency goes back to death of Harrison.

Ben. Burton and Francis Harrison Partners from 1700 to Harrison's death in 1725, during which time they laid out large sums in Purchase of Lands, Buildings, etc.

From 1701 to 23, Burton and Harrison divided in Profits £107,660. Bradshaw copy has by " R. Roberts " in MS.

234. A Second Letter From N-- N—, Creditor Of Burton's Bank, To A— C—, Esq;

Dublin : Printed in the Year M,DCC,LI.

8vo. 8 pp.

H.C.

Refers entirely to first letter and other published letter about the Creditors' Petition.

I have not been able to find the " First Letter," but the preceding number is the letter probably referred to.

A. C. was Abraham Creichton.

235. A Second Letter To The Creditors of Burton's Bank. From
a Person Conversant with the Affairs of that Bank, and no
Stranger to the interested Views, and scandalous Delays of
R. R. Esq; their Agent.
Printed in the Year 1752. (Dated Jan. (16) 1752.)
8vo. 15 pp. Signed X.Z.
H.C. 243.
Gives an Abstract of the Accounts.

236. A First Letter From R— R—s, Esq; To The Creditors of
Burton's Bank Containing, Part of his Answers to two Letters,
lately printed and addressed to them, and signed X.Z.
Dublin: Printed in the Year MDCCLII. (Dated Feb. 17th,
1752).
H.C. 243.
R. R. was R. Roberts.

237. A Letter To A Commissioner Of The Inland Navigation;
Concerning The Tyrone Collieries.
Dublin: Main, M,DCC,LII.
8vo. 23 pp.
H.C. 243.

238. The Irish Collieries And Canal defended, In Answer to a
Pamphlet, Entitled, A Letter To A Commissioner Of The
Inland Navigation, Concerning the Tyrone Collieries.
Dublin: G. and A. Ewing, M,DCC,LII.
8vo. 22 pp. Signed Publicola *i.e.* probably Thomas Dawson.
H.C. 243.

239. A Miscellany, Containing Several Tracts on Various Subjects.
By the Bishop of Cloyne. ....
Dublin: Faulkner. MDCCLII.
12mo. 264 pp.
(By George Berkeley).
Contains "The Querist."

240. Considerations On The Case Of The Bakers in Dublin. By
a Citizen.
Dublin: Printed and sold by the Booksellers. MDCCLII.
8vo. 31 pp.
Same, 2nd edition with Additions. By a Citizen.
Dublin: Ewing, 1752.
8vo. 34 pp.
H.C. 243.
A History of the Regulations, Weights of Bread, &c. since 1670.

241. Some Facts and Observations Relative to the Fate of the late Linen Bill, Last Session of Parliament In This Kingdom.
Dublin: Printed in the Year M,DCC,LIII.
8vo. 33 pp.
H.C. 249.
The bill as returned would have deprived Ireland of the privilege of sending linen to America.

242. A Dialogue Between Dean Swift and Tho. Prior, Esq; In The Isles of St. Patrick's Church, Dublin, On that memorable Day, October 9th, 1753.
By a Friend to the Peace and Prosperity of Ireland.........
Dublin: G. and A. Ewing, 1753.
8vo. 134 pp.

243. An Attempt To prove that a Free and Open Trade Between The Kingdom of Ireland And all the Ports of the Southern Coasts of England Would Be Highly Advantageous to both Kingdoms, etc., etc.
In a Letter to the Worshipful the Mayor and Chamber of The City of Exeter. By a truly impartial Hand.
Exon: Brice, 1753.
8vo. 44 pp.
U.C.—Hib. 7. 753. 2.
Denies that the decay of woollen manufactures in the West was due to smuggling of wool to France. Wool is not smuggled, and has not been for 30 years past, but if so it must be from Kent and Sussex. Nor was 1-1000 part of the wool smuggled from Ireland that people imagine. Smuggling now unpopular in Ireland, and the mob of combers would demolish the house of anyone suspected to be engaged in it. The eight sloops built to stop smuggling were never used on the Coast of England, because the Board of Customs knew none was smuggled, but were all sent to the Irish Coast, and never took a prize.
Some wool is smuggled out of the North of Ireland, and some worsted, but only trifling amounts.
Says the Books and Pamphlets written on this subject for many years preceding the resignation of Walpole, were written, published and industriously spread with no other view or design but to increase the popular clamour and resentment against the Administration. Since Walpole's resignation, scarcely a single Tract has appeared.

244. A Letter To His Excellency Henry Boyle, Esq. Speaker of the Honourable House of Commons in Ireland. With Remarks On The Linen Trade and Manufactures of the Kingdom, and some Hints for promoting the same.
Dublin: Faulkner, MDCCLIII.
8vo. 16 pp. (signed N. A.)
B.M. 1029, *b.* 6 (2).

245. An Account Of The Revenue And National Debt Of Ireland. With Some Observations on the late Bill for Paying off the National Debt. In which is contained, A Speech to the Parliament of Henry Lord Viscount Sidney, Lord Lieutenant in

the Year 1692, as also an Order of Council, and several Resolutions of the House of Commons, extracted from their Journals, parallel to the present Juncture of Affairs in that Kingdom.
London : Carpenter, 1754.
8vo. 48 pp. b.f.t.

246. Considerations On the late Bill For Payment of the Remainder Of The National Debt, In which the Occasion of inserting The Clause Relative To His Majesty's Consent,· And The Arguments in Support of such Right in the Crown, are impartially stated.
Dublin, printed : London, reprinted ; William Owen, M.DCC.LIV.
8vo. 60 pp.
(By Christopher Robinson).

This controversy, which was strictly a constitutional one, produced a large number of pamphlets, of which both the U.C. and H.C. have good collections.

247. Remarks On A Pamphlet Intitled, Considerations On the Late Bill For Paying the National Debt, etc.........
Dublin : Printed in the Year MDCCLIV.
8vo. 16 pp. (at end) Number I. The Remainder will be published in a few Days.

248. The Great Importance and Necessity Of Increasing Tillage, By An Act of Parliament, in Ireland, in Proportion to the Number of its Inhabitants. Demonstrated : Together, With the Usefulness and Advantages of erecting Public Granaries, and granting Premiums on the Exportation of Corn: In a Letter Addressed to the Right Honourable John, Earl Grandison......
Dublin : Wilson, MDCCLIV.
8vo. 52 pp. (signed Publicola).
Second edition. Same. MDCCLV.

Probably by Thos. Dawson, at least by same Publicola as A Dissertation in 1741.

249. The Universal Advertiser : Or, A Collection of Essays, Moral, Political and Entertaining : Together With Addresses from several Corporate and other Bodies in Ireland, To their Representatives in Parliament relative to their Conduct on the 23rd of November, and 17th of December, 1753. As also Compleat Lists of the Voters on both Sides, etc., etc.
Dublin : Dunn, 1754.
8vo. 250 pp. + 4 Index.

This paper contains some articles reflecting on the Government, written by Sir Richard Cox.

250. Considerations On The Present State Of The Linen Manufacture. Humbly addressed to the Trustees Of The Linen-Board.
Dublin : Printed in the Year MDCCLIV.
8vo. 32 pp.
H.C. 259.

251. A Dialogue Between A Banker And A Merchant Of The City
of Dublin.
   Dublin: Printed in the Year MDCCLIV.
   8vo.   8 pp.
   H.C. 259.

Seems the Treasury had issued a letter that it would pay out money
for banker's notes ; but the banker asserts they cannot do it without
enlarging their securities, and they will not do that.

Banker says one bank of no visible security broke, and an appearance
of a run on another, owing to its issue of small notes, which brought
a crowd, but total demands were trifling.   The bankers, nobility and
gentry and leading traders did not join in returning thanks to the
Governor for his so-called Interposition, which would imply there was
real danger.

252. An Inquiry Into The Causes Of Our Want of Tillage In Ireland : With Some Hints For Establishing a Yeomanry.
   By Michael Whyte, Gent.
   Dublin: Printed for the Author, MDCCLV.
   8vo.   31 pp.

253. A Letter To The People of Ireland ; On The Present State Of
The Kingdom.   Relative to the Banks, etc.
   By R. Sharp, Esq;   ....
   Dublin: Printed in the Year M.DCC.LV.
   8vo.   14 pp. (dated March 14).
   H.C. 259.

All the evils foretold of a public bank have been amply satisfied by
the private ones.

Thinks the profit derived from issuing notes should be used in supporting public credit.

Dublin, 3rd of March, 1755, a general subscription was signed by
many merchants, vouching for the safety of Gleadowe & Co., Kane &
Latouche, Mitchel & Macarell, R. & T. Dawson, T. Finlay & Co., and
on the same day these bankers issued a circular agreeing to accept each
other's notes as cash.

It seems, however, that some months before these same bankers had
issued a similar circular in conjunction with Willcocks & Dawson, who
had since failed, and now none of the others will take Willcocks &
Dawson's notes.   Estimates that £300,000 of Willcocks & Dawson's
notes are out, and therefore universal stagnation has ensued.   Proposes a
guarantee of some kind on these notes, so that they can at least pass at
that rate.

Proposes a public subscription by way of loan to pay off the pressing
demands on Willcocks & Dawson's Bank and keep it open.   Thinks
£50,000 sufficient.

254. Remarks On The Conduct Of Messrs. W — ks and D......n,
Late Bankers Of The City of Dublin, and Mr. R — d B — r
Their Cashier.
   By a Country Gentleman.........
   Dublin: G. Harrison (*n. d.*), *but* 1755.
   8vo.   60 pp.
   H.C. 259.

According to this W. & D. issued a statement on their failure, showing assets of £251,000, besides £70,000 due from their cashier, and
liabilities of £280,000 only.

The cashier, it seems, issued a statement, expressing surprise at the amount charged against him, but stating he would pay all he owed. On the 8th March the cashier was arrested. This pamphlet vindicates the cashier, and contains a complete statement of the proceedings in this case, from which it seems there were many irregularities immediately after the failure. Also seems their friends were let into the secret three or four days before, and succeeded in getting out most of their money.

First bank to fail in ten years was—
> *Lunell & Dickison* in 1745, but it was only a comparatively new bank, and satisfied all its creditors in a few months.

Second—*Dillon & Farril* in March, 1754.

Third—*Willcocks & Dawson*, who were Quakers, and on this account the bank had the greatest credit.

Fourth—*Lenox & French.* This failure due to W. & D.'s, and they are now paying off all notes under £20, and will soon settle in full.

Fifth—*French & Co.*, in Galway ⎫ General distrust in banks causing
Sixth—Lynch   ,,   ,, ⎭ a run.

According to an advertisement of June, W. & D. estimated the estate to produce 13s. 4d. in the pound, the liabilities being reduced to £192,000, and assets to £152,000, probably by accepting notes in payment of debts.

Insinuates that the failure was a long premeditated design, without any assignable excuse.

255. A Letter To The Creditors Of Messrs. W — ks and D — n, Late Bankers Of The City of Dublin.
> By the Author of the Remarks. ......
> *Dublin : Samuel (n. d., but* 1755).
> 8vo. 14 pp. (dated Naas, Sept. 24, 1755).
> *H.C.* 259.

Seems the Quakers took exception to the preceding pamphlet, and issued a statement in Faulkner's Journal of Sept. 13 denying all the accusations and refuting the insinuations contained in those remarks. Advertisement issued by the Society, but the writer says it is not a question of the Society, but of Quakers individually, and charges them with connivance and favoured treatment both before and after the failure.

Asserts as a fact that will be proved, that a Convention was held three days before the failure, attended by Quakers and a few others ; and during the last three days none of their friends passed-in anything, but most of them took out their deposits in specie.

256. Observations On The Conduct of Messrs. W — cks and D — n, Late Bankers Of The City of Dublin, Towards Mr. R — d B — r their Cashier.
> *Dublin : Samuel (n. d., but* 1755).
> 8vo. 8 pp.
> *H.C.* 243.

About Willcocks & Dawson's failure.

257. Burkitt's Observations On The Inland Navigation, etc., etc.
> *Dublin : Cotta,* MDCCLV.
> 8vo. 8 pp.
> *H.C.* 259.

258. A Reply To Some Assertions Published in a Pamphlet Entitled, The Scheme for Inland-Navigation from Dublin to the Shannon. With some Remarks relative thereto.
   By Matthew Peters.
   Dublin : Printed in the Year MDCCLV.
   8vo. 16 pp.
   H.C. 259.

259. Mr. Omer's Letter To The Public. Comptroller of the Inland Navigation.
   Dublin : Printed in the Year MDCCLV.
   8vo. 16 pp.
   H.C. 259.

260. A Letter To A Member of Parliament Concerning the Inland Navigation Of Ireland And The Many Advantages Arising from it.
   By Iernus Cambrensi.
   Dublin. Printed in the Year MDCCLV.
   8vo. 15 pp.
   H.C. 259.

261. An Essay On Coin. By Bryan Robinson, M.D.
   Dublin : Reilly, M.DCC.LVII.
   8vo. 104 pp.
   Originally published in 1737, but now enlarged and published by Dr. Robinson's sons.

262. Maxims Relative to the present State Of Ireland. 1757. Humbly submitted to the Consideration of the Legislative Powers.
   Dublin : Printed and sold by the Booksellers, MDCCLVII.
   8vo. 24 pp.
   H.C. 275.

   Chiefly on Neglect of Agricultural and Suspension of Land Improvement. Remarks on the effect of these on climates. Speaks of last six years of excessive rain, and consequent deterioration of coarse lands. Also on the Laws restricting Papists from investing in real securities.

263. A Proposal For the better Supplying the City of Dublin, With Corn and Flour ; Being, Heads of a Bill Intended to be laid before the Parliament, at their next Meeting.
   Dublin : Watts. MDCCLVII.
   8vo. 16 pp.
   H.C. 277.

264. A Letter From A Citizen of Dublin, To A Member of Parliament. Containing a Political Scheme For the Relief of the Poor of Ireland ; For easing the Nation of Beggars and other Burthensome Members ; and for increasing the Commerce

and Strength of His Majesty's Dominions, particularly the British Colonies in North America.

Dublin : Powell. MDCCLVII.

8vo. 40 pp. Signed Hibernicus.

H.C. 275.

Advocates settling these people in America, and allowing £20 for transporting and settling each person. This will settle there 30,000 people at a cost of £600,000, which is what the Author calculates it costs per annum to maintain this number in Ireland.

265. Hints For Erecting County Granaries In This Kingdom, As the sure Means to lower the exorbitant Price of Corn at the latter End of the Year ; To preserve a Sufficiency for homeward Consumption, to the great Relief of the Poor, And the Preservation of all our Manufactures. Addressed To The Right Honourable John Ponsonby, Speaker to the Hon. House of Commons. By Walter Weldon, Esq.

Dublin : Sleater, MDCCLVII.

8vo. 34 pp. b., t. and f. t.

H.C. 277.

266. A Proposal To prevent the Price of Corn from Rising too high, or Falling too low, by the Means of Granaries. By Thomas Prior, Esq.

8vo. 7 pp. Without regular title.

B.M. 8247. *b.* 36.

B.M. gives date as 1755, but it is the same as " A Proposal for Erecting Granaries," of 1741, and is probably a later reprint, most likely of 1757, when the Granary idea was again prominent.

267. An Inquiry Into The State and Progress Of The Linen Manufacture Of Ireland. In which will be introduced Remarks on the Principal Transactions of the Trustees of the Linen Board. To be Published Monthly.

Number I.

Dublin : Powell, MDCCLVII.

8vo. 208 pp. Dedication signed : Rob. Stephenson.

3 numbers in all.

Prefixed is : Consideration on The Present State of the Linen Manufacture. Humbly addressed to the Trustees of the Linen Board. Published in 1754.

B.M. 8244. *c.* 30.

Number I. gives an Extract from Crommelin's Essay. Very complete history of the Linen Trade with Notices of most of the authors, who had written on the subject.

Stephenson was a Linen Inspector.

268. Considerations On The Revenues Of Ireland. Shewing, The Right, Justice, and Necessity, of now applying the Duties granted them for guarding of the Seas, to Naval Services ; By Which Ireland will be certain of frequent Meetings of

Parliament, without paying £150,000 a Year for them as a favour.

London: Cooper, MDCCLVII.

8vo. 43 pp., b. t. and f. t.

B.M. 116. *g.* 10.

Refers to the great Increase of Wealth and Trade in Ireland as evidenced by the increase in Revenues collected from very low Duties. Most of the Revenue appropriated to local improvements and advantages, without any contributions to the Preservation of the whole or guarding the Seas.

269. Considerations On The Case Of The Bakers in Dublin. First published in the Year 1751, And now Reprinted, with Amendments and large Additions ; And A Proposal For A New Table of Assize.

Dublin: Ewings. MDCCLVII.

8vo. x. 58 pp.

H.C. 277.

270. Some Hints For the Advancement of Tillage, And for supplying the City of Dublin with Coals Constantly at a moderate Price. Humbly inscribed to the Right Honourable Hercules Langford Rowley, Esq. ....

Dublin: Sleater, MDCCLVIII.

8vo. 20 pp.

271. The Management Of The Revenue With Queries Relative Thereto. ....

Dublin: Printed in the Year MDCCLVIII.

8vo. 35 pp.

H.C. 282.

Letter published in 1755, in the Universal Advertiser.

272. Some Thoughts On The General Improvement Of Ireland, With A Scheme of a Society For Carrying on all Improvements In a more extensive and effectual Manner than has hitherto been done. Humbly submitted to the Consideration of the Right Honourable and Honourable The Lords and Commons, In Parliament Assembled.

Dublin: Powell. MDCCLVIII.

8vo. 49 pp.

H.C. 774.

Advises a National Bank.

A sure proof of the need of paper-money is the easy Credit any one procures, who sets up a Bank, notwithstanding Frauds and Insolvencies of Bankers.

A National Bank is therefore necessary, with Branches in the most convenient place of the other three Provinces. He means a truly National Bank, owned by the Nation and with all Profit to the public use, the notes to be Legal Tender.

Also suggests Granaries to keep Price of Wheat within reasonable bounds. Opposes bounties on exportation, but favours premiums for improvement and for supply of seeds, &c.

(71)

273. A Letter To The Right Honourable and Honourable The Trustees Of The Linen Manufacture. By Rob. Stephenson, Merchant.
Dublin: Hunter, 1759.
8vo. 1 sheet tables. 24 pp.
H.C. 290.

274. The Intentions Of Ireland Considered, Stated, And Recommended, Particularly with Respect to Ireland's Navigation.
Dublin: Faulkner. MDCCLIX.
8vo. 168 pp. (Ded. signed H. Brooke).
B.M. 8245. *e.* 59.

First Chapter on Money, Credit, &c., in which he says the Credit given to any Medium of Circulation is what alone constitutes the value thereof.
The Manufacturer alone raises and produces real wealth.
Chiefly devoted to improving Methods of Communication.

275. The Conduct of Messrs. Daniel Mussenden, James Adair, and Thomas Bateson, And the Other Managers Of The Belfast Charitable Scheme, Impartially Examined. ....
Printed in the Year M,DCC,LIX.
8vo. 40 pp.
H.C. 290.

Seems these gentlemen were Bankers in Belfast as well as Managers of the Scheme. Dispute growing out of a Lottery in aid of the Charity, which gave small results and left plenty of disputes behind.

276. The Clothier's Letter To The Inhabitants Of The Liberties.
Dublin: Printed in the Year MDCCLIX.
8vo. 16 pp. Signed Ab—W.
H.C. 289.

Panegyric on the Duke of Bedford's Administration, in giving premiums on land carriage of corn in 1757, restricting distillery, and penalizing the coal association.

277. Some Thoughts On The Nature Of Paper Credit, Relative to the late Failures of Bankers and Receivers in Ireland. By a Free-Citizen.
Dublin: Printed in the Year 1759.
8vo. 24 pp.
B.M. G. 4800. (2).

In this discusses the recent failures and the compositions offered, which he says are neither fair nor honourable. Speaks of the previous over-valuation of the quadruple pistoles at £3 13s., and says they were found to be 1/6 each short in the fineness, after £50,000 had passed into the hands of the people, but no one ever inquired who had introduced them.
Burton's bankruptcy has been 30 years in the Courts, and they finally, a few years ago, got an Act passed compelling the creditors to accept any settlement, if agreed to by two-thirds of them, although there was sufficient to pay in full, principal and interest.
Dillon's and Lenox's Banks each only paid out 2s. 6d. in the pound.
In a supplement proposes to issue a Government Loan of £350,000, and take the creditors' notes or receipts in payment of the subscription,

the estates of the defaulting bankers to be seized and to be converted into cash to pay off the Loan thus created.

Mitchell's assets £147,000, with supposed liabilities of £77,000. Malone's, Clements' and Gore's debts supposed to be £281,000, besides the deficiency of the cashier, Mr. Knight, of £71,000.

Thinks paper unnecessary and harmful, and says Ireland can get all the specie she requires.

Another edition. *Dublin.* 1760. 24 pp.

277ᵃ Paper-Credit Considered : Particularly Relative To the late Failures of Bankers and Receivers in Ireland. With A Scheme For supplying the broken Banks with Cash, and the Relief of their Sufferers.

Dublin Printed: London Reprinted, For Jonh Child. MDCCLX.

8vo. 35 pp.

B.M. 8225. *b.* 58.

May be imperfect, as it does not have the Scheme added in, but possibly never printed. Otherwise the same as the preceding number.

278. A Letter To The Author of a Pamphlet Entituled Some Thoughts On The Nature Of Paper Credit. ......

Dublin: Printed in the Year 1760.

8vo. 24 pp. Signed Publicola, dated Jan. 5th, 1760.

Probably by Thos. Dawson.

H.C. 298.

Claims that the notes and receipts (Mitchell and Malone's) pass in the Custom-House, and will be taken for goods and have some credit.

Denies that the invasion of the French was the cause, but the reduction of the gold in 1737. The effect of this was to drive foreign gold from the country (which produced 3 per cent. profit to the exporter) and make the trade of "Bankering" an absolute necessity, "and if there is no real money nor mint of our own, we must contrive imaginary or paper money." "So men of fortune and credit naturally become bankers, and, if prudent, like Hugh Henry, and Lunell and Dickisson, and only discount city notes and bills, they are of universal service. During twenty years only guineas imported, which became a subject of abuse, not being subject to weighing. Now bankers and traders, as a source of remedy, have agreed to weigh guineas in the future, and take only those of 5 dwt. 3 grs."

Denies the assertions about the quadruple moidore, and says very few were under value. The matter was misrepresented, and being lowered to £3 11s. were all exported, and he got 2s. 6d. premium on a considerable number he exported. Exportation a proof that they were now under-valued. Intimates that Exchange has been against Ireland frequently for past 20 years, leading to export of guineas and generally a run on the Banks.

Mitchell owed £70,000 and gave to Trustees £147,000 in Securities. Mitchell was a nephew of Hugh Henry, who gave him £300 a year to set up with. Also had the best remittances in Ireland at 1 per cent. profit, which would give him £6,000 per annum. Therefore nothing strange that he should collect £68,000 in 25 years.

According to this writer, Clements, Malone and Gore must have been possessed of large estates (he estimates them at £593,500) but apparently in land, offices, &c.

Dillon alone imported 300,000 guineas in 2 years, by which he lost £5,000, and they were exported as fast as imported. Says he kept bad accounts, neglected his affairs, and sent £40,000 to his brother in London and £5,000 to another in Holland. (Apparently first failure).

Willcocks' Bank of great use to the public for 40 years, and he lost £70,000 by a servant, with whom several men in trade had suspicious connections.

Lenox held forth in a public-house the night before his failure, and expressed great surprise at Willcocks, and canted an hour in favour of himself and a Banker's duty. Pretended he had lent £24,000 to a certain merchant, and that he was not possessed of a true worldly spirit of keeping, but his friends did not believe this.

What induced Malone and others to go into banking was the success of Lord Besborough and Mr. Gardiner on a former occasion. But then there was plenty of foreign coin in the kingdom, which could not be exported, until Exchange got to 12 per cent., which was rarely. Traders did not keep weighable money, and the Banks were full of money, and Besborough and Gardiner in particular had plenty, till they thought proper to pay off the public.

"Real Securities may in the eyes of the Law be better than Personal Securities, yet in the ways of the world, and for immediate payment it is not so. The Gentlemen of real estates may value their honours as they may please, but without punctuality it is of very little value."

279. The Draper's Ghost's Answer To The Clothier's Letter.
Dublin : Printed in the Year 1760.
8vo. 15 pp.
H.C. 298.
A few facts on the other side.

280. The New Bankers Proved Bankrupts, In a Dialogue between Themselves and a Free-Citizen. With some second Thoughts On The Nature Of Paper-Credit In Ireland.
Printed in the Year 1760.
8vo. 24 pp.
B.M. 8227. *aaa.* 22.
By the author of "Some Thoughts." An attack on Lord Russell, who he intimates was connected in some underground way with Malone and Gore.

281. Observations On And a Short History of Irish Banks And Bankers. By a Gentleman in Trade.
Dublin : Printed and Sold by the Booksellers, MDCCLX.
8vo. 40 pp.
H.C. 291.
While paper currency may be necessary, yet, even if the security be good, its over-issue leads to the enhancement of prices, wages, &c. and leads ultimately to an increase of imports and a decrease of exports.

Every evil that can arise from the monopoly of money has been produced by the private bankers. Indeed, the bad effects of paper are so pronounced, that the author thinks it likely it would be better to be reduced to the original stock of specie. On the whole prefers the establishment of a National Bank, otherwise the Parliament must establish private banking on a more secure footing.

The tract gives much information about Malone, Gore, and Clements' Bank, and the financial occurrences of the day.

282. A Letter From a Shop-Keeper In Dublin, To His Grace the Duke of Bedford, Lord Lieutenant of Ireland, &c. On Public Credit.

> *Dublin : Printed in the Year* 1760.
> 8vo. 16 pp.
> *H.C.* 291.

Paper Credit, either Foreign Bills of Exchange, Country-bills, Promissory notes—given for produce, and Bankers' notes. Computes current cash for 15 years past at £800,000, and Bank notes before the great Commotion at as much, and Bills and Promissory notes as three times as much. £400,000 in specie annually taken from Dublin to the North for the linen manufacture. Half of the Gold circulates in the North, and in the other parts of Ireland business chiefly by paper. More Gold now than ever, but not half the paper.

Banks are necessary, but too much money has been loaned to the landowners, and the difficulty of collection and delay in payment is the chief cause of the recent difficulties.

Bankers must confine themselves to Exchange and Discount.

283. Considerations On The Present Calamities Of This Kingdom ; And The Causes Of The Decay Of Public Credit With The Means Of Restoring It.

> *Dublin : Printed and sold by the Booksellers.* MDCCLX.
> 8vo. 15 pp.
> *H.C.* 298.

This Tract deals with the Banking business, suggesting certain legal restrictions limiting it to persons possessed of Estates of at least £40,000. The author proposes to forbid loans beyond 50 per cent. of the Capital, on Mortgages or any other Securities not realisable in six months, or loans at any time to more than double the amount of the Capital. He also suggests that Bankers be not allowed to follow any other business.

284. Proposals Humbly Offered To Parliament For The Restoration Of Cash And Public Credit To Ireland.

> *Dublin : Faulkner.* MDCCLX.
> 8vo. 15 pp.
>
> 2nd edition with Additions. Same year. 15 pp.
> *H.C.* 298.

Suggests raising again the Spanish and Portugal Gold coins and also Spanish Silver coins.

285. The Question Relative To The Petition Of The Cities of Dublin and Corke, and the Town of Belfast, For a new Regulation of the Portugal Gold Coin. Humbly addressed to the Publick, By a Citizen of Dublin. To which is added A Letter To The Merchants.

> *Dublin : Printed in the Year* MDCCLX.
> 8vo. 22 pp.
> *H.C.* 291.

The Scheme was to raise Portugal 40/- pieces from £1 18s. 10d. to £1 19s. and the large pieces from £3 17s. 8d. to £3 18s. (equivalent in Irish), the values at which they passed in England : the idea being that returns from Portugal will then be made in Specie instead of Bills on England. The author disputes this by saying, that inasmuch as the

Export of specie from Portugal is steadily prohibited, it can only be brought in Men of War and Packets, which naturally do not come to Ireland.

Advocates withdrawing the Proclamation fixing the value of Portugal coin, and permitting it to pass at its real value.

286. Reasons For And Against Lowering The Gold And Silver Of This Kingdom: Or rather to Estimate All Gold and Silver Here At the Price of Bullion, as we have No Mint: The Silver to be the Rule or Standard of Gold, as 1 to 15; that is 15 ounces of Silver to constitute the value of 1 Ounce of Gold: The Silver at 5s. 4d. and the Gold at 3l. 18s. 6d. per Ounce, English; which was the Average price of both, at a Medium, these ten Years last past.

In Three Letters directed to J. P. J. And One Letter to a Friend. And Humbly Inscribed and Dedicated to Hely Hutchinson, Esq. the Darling of the People, by his most obedient humble Servant, Publicola.

Dublin : Printed in the Year M,DCC,LX. (Dated May 5th-10th-15th).

8vo. 35 pp.

The Same. Humbly Inscribed and Dedicated To William Brownlow, Esq. ...... Part II.

Dublin : Printed in the Year M,DCC,LX.

8vo. 16 pp.

H.C. 298.

(Probably by Thos. Dawson).

In the first of these he attributes the large coinings of the English Mint after 1715 to the influx of foreigners, due to Marlborough's Exploits and the suppression of the Rebellion of 1715. Jews especially came in in large numbers.

Estimates cost of carrying money to and from England at 1 per cent. Insurance, and 1 per cent. Commission, freight, premium to captain, &c.

Suggests a Mint, the outlines of which were laid down by Mr. Simons.

Part II is, A Scheme For a Mint in Ireland, or at the Tower of London, for Ireland (which is by Mr. Simons).

287. Information To The People of Ireland, Concerning The Linen Trade Of Spain, Portugal and the Spanish West Indies. By C. S. Merchant.

Dublin : Watts. MDCCLX.

8vo. 16 pp.

H.C. 290.

288. An Essay On The Antient and Modern State Of Ireland, With The Various important Advantages thereunto derived, under the auspicious Reign of His most sacred Majesty King George the Second. Including A Particular Account of the great and glorious St. Patrick. ......

Dublin : Printed ; London re-printed for R. Griffiths MDCCLX.

8vo. 80 pp.

Much ancient and little modern, except a rather laudatory description of the products, learning, etc. of Ireland. Still deplores the great extent of pasturage, especially in the West.

289. The Case Of Edward Lord Bishop of Elphin, In Relation to Money, Part of the Rents of the Ranelagh Charity, lodged in a public Bank in Dublin. With Notes, Critical and Explanatory, By Sir Richard Cox, Bart.
> *Dublin : Wilson.*   MDCCLX.
> 8vo.   16 pp.
> *B.M.* 6345. *aa.* 2.

Lenox's Bank—afterwards Lennox and French—stopped Mar. 3, 1755. No economics, but a dispute on the Charity between Cox and the Bishop, Cox being the grandson of the original Trustee.

290. Some Considerations Relative to the Coal Trade In Dublin.
> *Dublin : Faulkner.*   MDCCLXI.
> 8vo.   12 pp.
> *H.C.* 302.

291. Some Hints For The better Improvement of Husbandry, And Reducing it to a Rational and Intelligible System.   In A Letter Humbly Submitted to the Consideration Of His Excellency the Right Honorable The Earl of Halifax Lord Lieutenant of Ireland, and President of the Dublin Society for the Encouragement of Husbandry, &c.   And the Rest of Members of that Respectable Body.
> *Dublin : Laurence Flin,* MDCLLXII.
> 8vo.   Title, iv.   86 pp.
> *U.C. Hib.* 7. 762. 4.

First tract in Ireland by John Wynn Baker.

292. Some Hints On Trade, Money and Credit : Humbly Addressed, To The True Friends Of Ireland.
> *Dublin : George and Alexander Ewing.*   M.DCC.LXII.
> 8vo.   24 pp.
> *B.M.* 8245. *aa.* 8.

Attributed in MS. on title of B.M. copy to Arthur Jones Neville (a Banker).

At time of writing says affairs, trade, &c. are in a thriving way.

Suggests Premiums to the home merchants and manufacturers, and thinks it was a mistake to have given the land-carriage bounty on corn, as it should have been coastwise to also support the shipping trade.

Things that although Banks are of late in disrepute, yet the certain good they do counterbalances a hundred-fold the Hazard of their Failure, which, he says, has always happened on account of their dealing with landed men or purchasing land.   By the use of Banks, a million circulated for many years, but paper now almost stopped.

From 1750 to 1755, and in part to 1759, Public Credit, or rather the confidence we had in each other, caused an overflow of circulating paper, which led to speculation and large imports, therefore the late stoppages, although distressful to particular persons, have been of real use to the Kingdom, by giving a check to a sort of credit, that had been carried to too great a length, and by experience we find no Bank can succeed unless calculated for and supported by the traders, and that now business is reduced to such a basis.

Winds up by urging that no monopoly of the coin of the Kingdom be permitted.

293. Some Short Historical Anecdotes, With Remarks Relative to Ireland. By George Stacpoole, Esq; In Four Parts. Part I.
Corke: Swiney, 1762.
8vo. 94 pp.
H.C. 308.
A general survey of trade and manufacture of Ireland.
Attributes luxury in Ireland to a want of trade.
Also surveys the trade and affairs of the world at large.

294. A Review Of The Evils That have prevailed in the Linen Manufacture Of Ireland.
Dublin: Wilson. MDCCLXII.
8vo. 45 pp.
H.C. 308.

295. The Present State Of His Majesty's Revenue Compared With that of some late Years.
Dublin: Wilson. MDCCLXII.
8vo. 15 pp. [By Sir Richard Cox.]
B.M. 8145. *aaa.* 5 (1).

296. Observations On a Paper intitled a Review Of The Evils That have prevailed in the Linen Manufacture Of Ireland.
Dublin: Printed in the Year 1762.
8vo. 8 pp.
H.C. 308.

297. A Hint For lessening the National Debt Of Great Britain.
Dublin: Wilson. MDCCLXII.
H.C. 309.
Scheme for depositing at birth of a child so much in a Bank, like those in Florence or Sienna. Ten times the amount to be paid, when the child reaches 18 years, and if it dies before, the money paid reverts to the Government.

298. The Golden Fleece: Or, Some Thoughts On The Cloathing Trade Of Ireland. With A Proposal for its Advancement, so far as to supply our own Consumption ; employ our idle Hands ; prevent their going for the future into France and Spain for Work ; and put an active Stop to the clandestine Exportation of Wool. By John Long, Clothier.
Dublin: Dyton. 1762.
8vo. 40 pp.
H.C. 308.

299. Impartial Considerations On The Danger Of Multiplying Banks here ; How far they may be Injurious to Trade, and Commerce, affect the Merchant and Manufacturer, and consequently the Landed Interest of This Kingdom. ....
By a Member of the Guild of Merchants, and a real Lover of his Country.
Dublin: Chamberlaine. MDCCLXIII.
8vo. iv-16 pp.
The author thinks affairs are in a more flourishing state than when

there were twice as many banks, and thinks Ireland has now a sufficient number of bankers.

The extension of the paper currency creates a competition to loan the notes and leads to increase of luxury and over-trading.

Written to oppose the introduction of a new bank, proposed to be started by two Londoners and a Dublin man.

This is the only copy of this tract that I have seen.

300. Reasons, Humbly Offered to Public Consideration ; Against The Present Scheme Of Reducing the Interest of Money In Ireland.
   Dublin : Ewing.   M,DCC,LXV.
   8vo.   45 pp. *b. t.*
   B.M. 8227. *aaa.* 20.

   Speaks as if the prospect of a National Bank was being agitated.

   Says the circulation of the money of the Kingdom is augmented and improved by the Banker's note, which becomes a real *implement of industry.*

   Instances exchange in 1745, on the run on the Banks in London ; bills passed in Dublin on London at 5 per cent. discount, but came over from London at 11-12 per cent.

   The Irish Bankers in time of danger (no doubt 1757-9), brought over specie from London instead of issuing their notes for bills in Dublin and remitting the bills.

   An unnatural rise in the price of lands, caused by cheap money, is pernicious.

   In considering the relative rate of interest in different countries, the climate and constitutions are to be taken into account.

   Very interesting tract, probably written by a Banker.

301. The Act For permitting the Free Importation of Cattle From Ireland, Considered with a View to the Interests of both Kingdoms.
   London.   Dodsley.   1765.
   8vo.   48 pp.
   H.C. 325.

   In the form of queries like the Querist.

302. Considerations On The Present State Of The Silk Manufacture In Ireland.
   Humbly submitted to the Members of both Houses of Parliament and the Dublin Society.   By A Lover of his Country.
   Dublin : Printed in the Year MDCCLXV.
   8vo.   16 pp.
   H.C. 325.

303. A Scheme For Establishing County Poor-Houses, In The Kingdom Of Ireland.   Published by Order of the Dublin Society.
   Dublin : Powell & Son.   MDCCLXVI.
   8vo.   15 pp.
   Second Edition of same, 1768.
   H.C. 332.

(79)

304. Reasons Against passing into a Law A Bill now depending in Parliament For Erecting Public Granaries in Dublin, Corke, and Belfast. With A New Plan For the Improvement of Tillage in Ireland, Humbly proposed to the Legislature.
Dublin : Potts. MDCCLXVI.
8vo. 16 pp.
H.C. 332.

Proposes a law to assist farmers to erect private granaries or haggards.

305. A Letter From Richard In The Country, To Dick In The City on The Subject Of Publick Granaries.
Dublin : Printed in the Year MDCCLXVI.
8vo. 15 pp.
H.C. 332.

306. An Essay To State Some Arguments Relative To Publick Granaries, Submitted with all Humility To The Nation Which They concern.
Dublin : MDCCLXVI.
8vo. 22 pp.
H.C. 332.

307. The Case fairly stated Relative To An Act, Lately Passed in this Kingdom Against The Exportation of Corn.
By a Friend to the Country.
Dublin : Printed in the Year MDCCLXVI.
8vo. 16 pp.
H.C. 332.

A discussion of the constitutional Power involved.

308. Quaeries Proposed to the Consideration of the Public, On the Reduction of the Interest of Money In Ireland.
Dublin : Sleater, 1766.
8vo. 16 pp.
B.M. 8227, *aaa.* 21.

Familiar idea of a nation getting rich by the balance of trade bringing in gold and silver.

Merchants and Farmers both greatly trading on credit. They pay the highest rates that can be lawfully demanded ; £100 4 per cent. Irish Funds worth now 107, although English 4 per cent. only 103.

A late Bank issued its notes at 2½ per cent., and lent money on real security at 5 per cent.

Interest reduced in 1704 to 8 per cent., and in 1732 to 6 per cent.

Land and produce now worth double what they were in 1732, although the value of lands has only increased 10 per cent.

Estimates population as 300,000 more than 1704, and 150,000 more than 1732.

Calls capitalists drones.

309. Seasonable Queries. Humbly Submitted To The Serious Consideration Of The True Friends of Ireland.
> *n. d. n. p.* but undoubtedly Dublin. No regular title.
> 8vo. 41 queries on 8 pp.
> *B.M.* 116, *g.* 40.

Suggests Tillage Act, Granaries, Work Houses, Tax on Absentees, Longer Leases, increasing Common Labourers' Wages. Reprobates the Rioters, Whiteboys, etc., destruction of corn, etc. by fire, and suggests levying a penalty of double damages on the Barony within which outrages occur.

Also animadverts on large farms and the land jobbers, the state of the Public Lights in Dublin, &c.

Bradshaw copy suggests 1766 as the date of this.

310. A List Of The Absentees Of Ireland. &c.
> *Dublin : Printed by Jones for Faulkner.* MDCCLXVII.
> 8vo. 75 pp. + Table.
> Second Edition, Corrected To which is Added an Appendix.
> *Dublin: Faulkner.* MDCCLXVII.
> 8vo. 80 pp. + Table.
> *H.C.* 336.

Third edition in 1769 by Faulkner, with notes, etc., since publication of former editions of 1767, in 102 pp., 4 folding tables. (Notes by Redmond Morres, Esq.)

In the beginning of this, says great stringency of money in Ireland in the summer of 1767, when Exchange rose to 10 per cent., merchants could not get bills discounted at any rate, and money on real security had risen from 4 per cent. to 6 per cent., and difficult to get at that, as bankers refused to lend money except on bills. Asserts that on this account they begin to consider the relaxation of the laws against allowing Papists to take real and landed security.

311. Two Letters To The Dublin Society.
> The First Proposing The Encouragement of a Manufacture, And The Second Of A Commerce. By Sir James Caldwell, Baronet, Fellow of the Royal Society.
> *Dublin : Powell.* MDCCLXVII.
> 8vo. 24 pp.
> *H.C.* 339.

Proposes a Premium for introducing plating and grinding of iron, and for encouraging fishing trade on the inland waters.

Some remarks on the growth of Dublin, rise in prices, &c.

312. An Argument In Support Of The Right Of The Poor In The Kingdom of Ireland, To A National Provision ; In the Appendix to which, An Attempt is made to settle a Measure of the Contribution due from Each Man to the Poor, on the Footing of Justice. By Richard Woodward, LL.D., Dean of Clogher. ......
> *Dublin : Powell.* MDCCLXVIII.
> 8vo. Ded. Adv. to the Reader. 55 pp.
> Re-issued in 1772.

313. Some Considerations To Shew The Utility Of An Immediate Reduction of Interest by Law from 6 to 5 per Cent.
By a Merchant. ....
Dublin : Exshaw. MDCCLXVIII.
8vo. 34 pp. (By Sir Lucius O'Brien).
B.M. 8145, *aaa.* 96.

Says the Irish 4 per cent. Funds at the time were worth 106½, and yet land sold for only 23 years' purchase.
Formerly wages in Ireland 3d. per day, and now one shilling.

314. Considerations On The Dependencies of Great-Britain. With Observations On A Pamphlet, Intitled The Present State of the Nation.
London : Printed.
Dublin : Re-printed for J. Williams .... MDCCLXIX.
8vo. 94 pp.

Very valuable and ably written pamphlet, chiefly devoted to Ireland, supposed to have been written by Sir Hercules Langrishe.
Largely quoted by Lecky.

315. To His Excellency The Right Honourable Lord Viscount Townshend, Lord Governor and Governor General of Ireland, President &c. The Dublin Society, The following Remonstrance is Most Humbly Addressed By John Wynn Baker.
Dublin : Powell. M,DCC,LXIX.
Sm. 8vo. 104 pp.
U.C. Hib. 7. 749. 22.

Contains some Autobiography. Came to Ireland in 1761.
First Publication: "Hints on Husbandry. (Flinn, 1762)." Took a Farm March 1763, and in Jan. 1764 Faulkner published for free distribution a sketch of his Plan. Elected Member of the Dublin Society in 1764, but resigned on receiving £100 from them to encourage his work. Order to pay him £100 April 5th, 1765, to recompense him for trouble in experimenting in culture of turnips, cabbage, spring wheat, &c. Reported to them Feb. 1765. 1765 Report printed and £200 more voted.
Remainder of Tract devoted to a Statement of his further Relations with the Society and accounts.

316. Some Observations On The Circumstance of Ireland.
n. p. n. d. (In March 1769. By Rev. Dr. Dennis?).
8vo. 16 pp.
U.C. Hib. 7. 769. 11.
Praying for the Relaxation of the Trade Restrictions in Ireland.

317. Letters Written By His Excellency Hugh Boulter, D.D. Lord Primate of All Ireland, &c. To Several Ministers of State in England, And Some Others. Containing An Account of the

most interesting Transactions which passed in Ireland from
1724 to 1738. Volume the First.
Dublin : Faulkner & Williams. MDCCLXX.
8vo. In 2 vols. Vol. I. viii, 288 pp. Vol. II. 198 pp. +
13 pp., Index.
The great authority on Ireland of the period.
First published in Oxford, 1769-70, as the letters were then deposited
in Christ Church, Oxford.

318. Serious Thoughts Upon A Subject Truly interesting to the
Welfare of Ireland, Submitted to the Consideration of both
Houses of Parliament ; but more particularly to the Country
Gentlemen.
By a Friend to the Yeomanry.
Printed in the Year, 1771.
8vo. 14 pp.
H.C. 361.
On the distillation laws, smuggling, and prices and effects of
spirituous liquors.
Advocates lowering the revenue duty.

319. Considerations Upon The Exportation of Corn ; Written At
The Request Of The Dublin Society.
By John Wynn Baker, F.R.S.
Dublin : Powell. MDCCLXXI.
8vo. 48 pp.
H.C. 366.
Re-printed in 1774 in Cork by Phineas Bagnell, in 48 pp.

320. An Address To The Representatives Of The People, Upon
Subjects of Moment to the Well-Being and Happiness Of
The Kingdom of Ireland. By a Friend to the Nation.
Dublin : Printed and sold by the Booksellers. MDCCLXXI.
8vo. 45 pp.
H.C. 361.
On the manufactures of Ireland, especially Silk, Woollen and Linen,
and concludes that the Fishery, Agriculture and the Linen Manufacture
are the only objects which should gain the primary attention of the
Kingdom.

321. Proposals Humbly offered to His Excellency Lord Townshend
And to the Present Parliament, For The Improvement of
Trade, And Restoration of Cash and Public Credit To Ire-
land, Now sinking for Want of Trade, and her late Troubles
in the North of Ireland.
Dublin : Hunter. M,DCC,LXXII.
8vo. 16 pp. Signed Publicola.
U.C. Hib. 7. 772. 19.
Thinks the Suppression of Spanish Coin and the Reduction of Portugal
Coin of unhappy consequence to Ireland, and also to England, since the
circulating medium must be derived from them. " Therefore all our
Bankruptcies, Failure of Public Credit, and of Trade and Business."
In 1760 the Banks that failed offered all their Securities as security

for the loan of Coin, "but could not get it, because there was none to be had. They could no more Mint their fortune than their Pavements."

Proposes restoring Spanish Coins (raising the piece of Eight to 5/-) and their Sub-denominations, "which are also far better coins than our present 12d. and 6d."

The Trade between England and Ireland consists in a kind of Barter of mutual redundancies for the supply of mutual wants.

For ⅓ of the year, Exchange in favour of Ireland, and British money imported.

For ⅔ of the year, Exchange against Ireland, and British money exported.

Fixed Exchange 8⅓ per cent., or £100 English = £108 6s. 8d. Irish.

Proposes raising Portugal Piece of Gold of 18 dwt. 10½ gr. from £3 17s. 8d. to £4 4s. ; that Spanish Milled Cobs, 17 dwt. 8 gr., be restored, and that Spanish Milled Piece of Eight, 17 dwt. 8 gr. (present currency 4/9), be raised to 5/-.

No silver coined at the English Mint for 12 years, most of the shillings being coined at Birmingham and Sheffield, and not worth 9½d. each.

In the Bradshaw copy there is a MS. note giving initials of author as E. (or P.) W., but as it embodies the same ideas as a "Letter to the Author" of 1760, it is certainly the same "Publicola," i.e. probably Thomas Dawson.

322. **Serious Considerations On The Present alarming State Of Agriculture And The Linen Trade.   By a Farmer.**
Dublin : Watson.   MDCCLXXIII.
8vo.   40 pp.
H.C. 361.

On Rents.   Suggests direct leases to the tenants, who work the farms, at a moderate rental of 13/- or 14/- per acre, abolishing duty work, mill duty, &c. &c.

323. **Plan Of An Universal Fishing Company In Ireland.**
Dublin : Husband.   MDCCLXXIII.
8vo.   32 pp.
H.C. 361.

324. **A Letter To The Universal Fishing Company Of The Kingdom of Ireland.   By Henry Brooke, Esq.**
Dublin : Williams.   MDCCLXXIII.
8vo.   18 pp.
H.C. 361.

325. **A Letter Upon The Subject Of Taxing The Estates Of Absentees.**
Dublin : Printed in the Year MDCCLXXIII.
8vo.   8 pp.
H.C. 361.

326. **Letters Which Passed In Great Britain Relative To The Absentee Tax.**
Dublin : Printed in the Year MDCCLXXIII.
8vo.   14 pp.
H.C. 361.

327. Remarks On The Decay Of The Linen Manufacture Of Ireland ; With Methods proposed for its Re-establishment and farther Improvement.
> By a General Trader, and a Traveller.
> *Dublin : Spotswood.* MDCCLXXIV.
> 8vo. vi. 25 pp.
> *H.C.* 381.
>
> Speaks of extraordinarily high prices for linen every third year in Cadiz on sailing of the Flota.

328. Report From The Committee Appointed To Consider Of The Methods practised in Making Flour from Wheat ; The Prices thereof ; And how far it may be expedient to put the same again under the Regulations of an Assize.
> *Dublin : Faulkner.* MDCCLXXIV.
> 8vo. 95 pp.
> *H.C.* 381.
>
> A reprint of a number of interesting documents, including " The Case of the Baker, the Mealman, and the poor Labourer, Stated," by T. Pownall.

329. Some Thoughts On The Present State Of The Linen Trade Of Great Britain and Ireland.
> *London.* 1774.
> 8vo. 22 pp.
> *H.C.* 381.

330. An Essay Concerning The Establishment Of A National Bank In Ireland.
> *London : Robinson.* MDCCLXXIV.
> 8vo. 51 pp. b. t.
>
> In a Letter to the Earl Nugent, 1780, John Gray, the author, says he wrote the above Tract.
> See No. 343 for Dublin reprint.

331. An Address To The Publick, On The Expediency Of A Regular Plan In The Maintenance And Government Of The Poor : In Which its Utility with respect to Industry, Morrals, and Publick Oeconomy is proved from Reason ; and confirmed by the Experience of the House of Industry lately established in Dublin. With Some General Observations on the English System of Poor Laws; and, an Examination of the Chapter in Lord Kaims's Sketch of the History of Man relative to the Poor. ....
> By Richard Woodward, LL.D., Dean of Clogher, and Chancellor of St. Patrick's, Dublin.
> *Dublin : Marchbank,* MDCCLXXV.
> 8vo. 91 pp.
> *H.C.* 387.

332. Commerce Not A Fit Subject For An Embargo. By An Eminent Barrister, Member of the late Parliament, etc.
Dublin : Walker, MDCCLXXVII.
8vo. 44 pp.
H.C. 401.
A strong attack on the justice and expediency of the embargo.

333. The Neglected Wealth of Ireland Explored. Or A Plain View of the Great National Advantages Which May Be Obtained By Completing The Navigation Of The River Shannon, The Uniting Of Other Rivers To It, The Working of Mines, And The Establishment Of Various Manufactures In The Kingdom of Ireland. etc., etc.
By J. C.
Dublin. Mills, MDCCLXXVIII.
8vo. 46 pp.
H.C. 402.

334. A Linen Draper's Letter To The Friends Of Ireland.
Dublin : Printed in the Year M.DCC.LXXVIII.
8vo. 27 pp.
H.C. 402.

335. Hints Preparatory To The Serious Consequences and Disadvantages of the Sundry Fisheries Of This Kingdom, Most Humbly Addressed To His Excellency John Earl of Buckingham Lord Lieutenant General and Governor General of Ireland : etc., etc., etc.
Dublin : Exshaw, MDCCLXXVIII.
(By Charles Grossett).
8vo. 71 + 3 pp.
H.C. 402.

336. Two Letters From Mr. Burke To Gentlemen In The City of Bristol, On The Bills Depending In Parliament Relative to the Trade of Ireland.
London : Dodsley, MDCCLXXVIII.
8vo. 32 pp.

337. Considerations On The Silk Trade of Ireland. With Useful Hints For The Extension Thereof, Addressed to the Dublin Society.
Dublin : Printed in the Year MDCCLXXVIII.
8vo. 30 pp.
H.C. 402.

338. A Comparative View Of The Public Burdens Of Great Britain And Ireland. With A Proposal for putting both Islands on an Equality, in Regard to the Freedom of Foreign Trade.
London : Printed, And Dublin : Reprinted by R. Burton, MDCCLXXIX.
8vo. 64 pp.
H.C. 415.

MS. note says : Printed in London in 1774, although Lecky gives date of London edition as 1779.

Very well written tract, frequently quoted by Lecky.

From internal evidence I believe this tract to have been written by the author of a Commercio-Political Essay on the nature of the balance of foreign trade, etc., printed in London by John Stockdale about 1787, and in a MS. Index to the volume containing that tract said to be by " Mr. Gray," no doubt John Gray, LL.D., who was Secretary to the Duke of Northumberland in Ireland in 1763-4.

I have never seen the original London edition of this tract, but believe it to have been published in 1772 as given in one of Rodd's catalogues.

339. Substance of Political Debate On His Majesty's Speech, On The Address, And The Amendment ; November 25th, 1779. With Remarks On The State Of The Irish Claim To A Fair Trade.

By a Volunteer.

London : Faulder, MDCCLXXIX.

8vo. 36 pp.

H.C. 411.

340. Terms of Conciliation Or, Considerations On A Free Trade in Ireland ; On Pensions On The Irish Establishment ; And On An Union with Ireland. Addressed To His Grace, the Duke of Northumberland.

London : MDCCLXXIX.

8vo. xxii. 68 pp. (signed Cincinnatus).

H.C. 418.

341. Thoughts On The Inexpediency Of Continuing The Irish Woollen Ware-House, As A Retail Shop, Humbly Offered To The Consideration Of The Members Of Both Houses Of Parliament And Those Of The Dublin Society In Particular.

Dublin : Wogan, 1779.

8vo. 19 pp.

H.C. 411.

342. Thoughts On The Present Alarming Crisis Of Affairs : Humbly Submitted To The Serious Consideration Of The People Of Ireland. Dedicated To The Right Honourable Lord Naas. To Which Are Added Two Letters, Formerly Written To The Popish Inhabitants Of This Kingdom. By a Grazier. ......

Dublin : Spotswood, MDCCLXXIX.

8vo. 31 pp.

H.C. 411.

On the prohibitory and restrictive laws, deprecating the agitation against them.

343. An Essay Concerning The Establishment Of A National Bank In Ireland.

Dublin : Hallhead, MDCCLXXIX.

8vo. 58 pp.

H.C. 418.

(By John Gray).

A discussion of the effect of the National Debt, ridiculing the idea that the capital is any fund. The only thing is the right to the interest, which is bought and sold.

Perennial sources of income are incomes from land and the industries of the people.

The bank proposed was to be a Government bank of £1,000,000, which would be issued in notes, £200,000 in specie to be withdrawn from circulation to provide for the convertibility of the notes. The notes to be lent on real security at 3 per cent.

Says over 30 issuers of paper in London alone.

Reprint of 1774 London edition.

344. Cursory Observations On Ireland. By A Member Of The Dublin Society.

Dublin: Faulkner, 1779.

8vo. 63 pp. [In MS. by Sir John Hasler.]

H.C. 417.

Attack on Irish landlords and plea for the peasants.

Proposes an Absentee Tax, and gives details of Irish productions, including some statistical observations in an appendix. Estimates inhabitants at 2,333,563, and asserts not one-fifth of the Irish eat bread. Estimates specie in Ireland at 3 millions.

345. Renovation Without Violence Yet Possible.

Dublin: Hallhead, MDCCLXXIX.

8vo. 46 pp.

H.C. 411.

Exceedingly interesting tract, proposing Imperial Federation of all the Colonies with Great Britain (Ireland included), with an Imperial Parliament ; every part maintaining its distinct Parliament and raising its local taxes, as well as a quota for the Imperial expenses. Perfect free trade between all parts ; with a religious establishment so liberal as to leave but few dissentients, and ample toleration.

America, exclusive of Canada, to be divided into three provinces. The Rotten Boroughs in the House of Commons to be lopped off to make room for the new members. The English members alone to sit on purely local questions.

346. A Letter To The People Of Ireland On The Expediency And Necessity Of The Present Associations In Ireland, In Favour Of Our Own Manufactures. With Some Cursory Observations On The Effects Of A Union.

Dublin: Colles, MDCCLXXIX.

8vo. 74 pp.

H.C. 411.

347. A Letter To William Eden, Esq; on The Subject Of His Excellency The Earl of Carlisle ; The Irish Trade.

By Richard Sheridan, Esq., of the City of Dublin, Barrister at Law.

Dublin: M. Mills. MDCCLXXIX.

8vo. 37 pp.

H.C. 415.

348. The Commercial Restraints Of Ireland Considered In A Series of Letters To A Noble Lord. Containing An Historical Account Of The Affairs Of That Kingdom So Far As They Relate To This Subject. ......
    Dublin. Hallhead. MDCCLXXIX.
    8vo. xxii. 240 pp. 3 Tables Appendix.
    (By Provost John Hely Hutchinson).
    There are several subsequent editions of this well-known work.

349. Guatimozin's Letters On The Present State Of Ireland And The Right of Binding it by British Acts Of Parliament, etc. ....
    London : Johnson. MDCCLXXIX.
    8vo. 76 pp. (Fred. Jebb, M.D.)
    B.M. T. 771. (5).

    A later edition, same year.
    The Letters Of Guatimozin, On The Affairs of Ireland, As First Published In The Freeman's Journal, And Which Having Been Since Re-Printed in London, Have Gone Through Several Editions There. To Which Are Added, The Letter Of Causidicus, That Accompanied The Essays of Guatimozin In Their First Appearance.
    Dublin : Marchbank. MDCCLXXIX.
    8vo. 82 pp. b. t. and f. t.
    Dr. Jebb made himself so disagreeable to the Government by his Letters, that he was bought off with a pension of £300 a year for his life and that of his wife. He apparently died in 1781-82.

350. An Enquiry How Far The Restrictions laid upon the Trade of Ireland, by British Acts of Parliament, are a Benefit or Disadvantage to the British Dominions, &c. &c.
    With An Address to the Gentlemen Concerned in the Woollen Commerce of Great Britain &c. &c. To which is Prefixed A Letter to Sir John Duntze Bart. M.P. for Tiverton on the same subject : in which a Union between the two Kingdoms is discussed. By Sir James Caldwell, Bart. Count of Milan in the Holy Roman Empire.
    Dublin : Marchbank. MDCCLXXIX.
    8vo. 100 pp.
    H.C. 418.

    Another edition.
    Exeter, Mugg. MDCCLXXIX.
    8vo. xii-113 pp.

351. Observations On The Finances And Trade Of Ireland; Humbly Addressed To The Immediate Consideration Of Gentlemen Of Landed Interest, More Particularly To Members Of The House Of Commons.
    n. d. n. p. (In MS. 1779, but in the Bradshaw Collection, bound in with 1775 Tracts).

8vo.   45 pp.
H.C. 415.

A scheme for a new system of taxation, borrowed from Decker, of licenses, based on external evidences of fortune.

352. The First Lines Of Ireland's Interest In the Year One Thousand Seven Hundred and Eighty.
Dublin.   Marchbank.   MDCCLXXIX.
8vo.   79 pp.
H.C. 411.

A general State of the Trade, Commerce, Manufactures, &c. of Ireland and System of Taxation.

353. A Dissertation On the Present Bounty Laws, For the Encouragement Of Agriculture In Ireland.
Submitted To The Consideration of Parliament.
Dublin : Hallhead.   MDCLXXX.
8vo.   31 pp.   (2 folding-tables, paged).
H.C. 426.

354. A View Of The Present State Of Ireland, Containing Observations Upon The Following Subjects, Viz. Its Dependance, Linen Trade, Provision Trade, Woolen Manufacture, Coals, Fishery, Agriculture, Of Emigration ; Import Trade of the City of Dublin, Effect of the Present Mode of Raising the Revenue on the Health and Happiness of the People, The Revenue, A National Bank ; and an Absentee Tax. Intended for the Consideration of Parliament, on the approaching Enlargement of the Trade of that Kingdom.   To which is added &c. &c. &c.
London.   Faulder.   MDCCLXXX.
8vo.   viii. 126.

Another edition.
Dublin : Fay.   MDCCLXXX.
8vo.   viii-126.
Slightly different title.

Also A Letter to the People of Ireland, In which are included Some Cursory Observations on the Effect of a Union.
London.   Faulder.   MDCCLXXX.
8vo.   74 pp.

355. Thoughts On A Fund For The Improvement Of Credit In Great Britain ; And The Establishment Of A National Bank In Ireland.
London : J. Murray, MDCCLXXX.
8vo.   33 pp.   b. t.
B.M. 104. c. 41.
Same.   By a Friend To Ireland In The British Parliament.
Dublin : Mills. MDCCLXXX.
8vo.   31 pp.

Thinks that paper issued as representative for really valuable property by its nature immovable, will in circulation not produce a disproportion between prices of things, and the value of the means with which they are purchased. Such a fabric cannot be weakened by too great extension.

Duties laid upon land by transferring a part of the property to others would establish as firm a basis for public credit as an equal proportion of soil pledged for the security of a National Bank, whilst free from any objections to which that plan is liable.

Suggests an unlimited right to establish Banks by holders of funds, who can issue notes against same, and prohibiting at the same time anybody from engaging in the banking business, except holders of stock, and such paper to be confined to the amount of stock held; (that is an indefinite extension of the privilege of the Bank of England to any person).

Calls attention to the paper mints, established even in paltry villages.

Above scheme would steady the price of stocks.

Contemplates extending this privilege to incorporated companies, and therefore advocates no present change until the Bank's charter expires in six years. But in Ireland the scheme can at once be put into effect.

Suggests £500,000 as sufficient, and that the debentures, now 13 per cent. discount, be the Irish Stock, to be subscribed.

Seems some other scheme (says a faint and inefficient essay) was in agitation in Ireland.

Charter should provide, that interest of 5 per cent. only should be charged, and that interest on the debentures (now 4 per cent.), might be reduced to 3 per cent., in consideration of the banking profit.

Any other scheme involves raising a loan of £500,000 in England, at an interest exceeding 7½ per cent.

All connexion with the Government to be forbidden, whether in public loans or any other monetary intercourse not absolutely necessary.

Out of the 5 per cent. interest, 2 per cent. would pay the expenses, and loss of interest of deposits reserved for payment at sight.

Estimates net profit to subscribers at least 8 per cent.

Appendix contains draft of certain provisions relative chiefly to the payment of interest on the Government stock.

Bank to be forbidden to lend money on landed security.

May be by John Gray.

356. Considerations On The Expediency Of A National Circulation Bank At This Time In Ireland. By Fred. Jebb, M.D., Author of Some Essays Lately Published Under the Signature of Guatimozin.

Dublin: Marchbank, MDCCLXXX.

8vo. 34 pp.

B.M. 8145. *d.* 56.

States that his arguments are based on Adam Smith's Treatise.

Quantity of paper-money must never exceed the amount of specie, which, without it, would necessarily have circulated in the country; as it is only applicable to home circulation.

Paper does not augment the capital of a country.

In foot-note, says the Directors of the Bank of England once found, that for some years they had to coin annually £800,000 to 1 million to answer the demands of cash for their notes, which, when carefully inquired into, was found to arise from a comparatively small excess in the circulation.

In 1780, the Irish Banks could not find eligible commercial bills sufficient for their capitals.

Recites the complaints against the private Banks, which are narrow and capricious, issuing heavily sometimes and nothing at other times. Gives most of the arguments for Private against Company Banks.

357. Some Remarks on Dr. Jebb's Considerations On The Expediency Of A National Circulation Bank In Ireland.

Dublin: Hunter. MDCCLXXX.

8vo. 24 pp.

H.C. 426.

According to general opinion, no person in the Banking Trade put in as a capital stock and permitted such capital to remain untouched for that purpose, above £10,000. Therefore, supposing there were 6 partners, there would be no more than £60,000 capital.

Of all the Banks in Ireland, only two of the present have been able to weather the storm (Mr. Henry, and Messrs. Coates & Lawless having honourably retired).

Quotes " Survey of the present State of Ireland," chapter on Banks.

358. A Letter To The Earl Of Nugent, Relative to the Establishment Of A National Bank In Ireland.

London: Donaldson. 1780.

8vo. 31 pp. Signed John Gray.

H.C. 426.

Restating the principles advocated in his " Essay Concerning the Establishment of a National Bank in Ireland."

Speaks of a correspondence with Nugent on this subject two years before. Bankers—instead of promoting cheaper rates for money, which has been the chief idea of the public in tolerating them—have sought to monopolise the profitable trade of money issuing. Within 30 years, however, traders have begun to fathom the mystery of the profit of the thing, and have set up everywhere mints of their own. Intimates that the Bank of England tried to ruin the first issuers in London of circulating notes, by running on them, but proving unsuccessful, they gave it up. Speaks of the immense advantages the American Colonies derived from coining their own money of paper on the National Credit.

Thinks the lack of employment in Ireland one of the chief causes of distress, rather than the want of a foreign vent for industry.

50 Banks have been established in 30 years past in Great-Britain, and notes already preferred to cash.

Thinks the offer of interest at 3 per cent. would greatly stimulate industry in Ireland.

In Scotland notes almost bear an agio in circulation, as the common people prefer them, having no question of their security.

The Dublin monied men had lately published resolutions asking the Government to give them gratis the Public Credit for them to lend to others, and even at a high interest to the Government itself. It is not only paper money that is likely to be raised and lowered, but even gold and silver, and the great Preventative is Stability of Regulations.

359. The Propriety of Extending The Trade of Ireland ; And The Advantages That Will Thereby Accrue To The Manufactures Of England, And The State in General.

By One of His Majesty's Commissioners For Trade And Plantations.

To Which Is Added, An Enquiry Into The Legality And

Consequences Of An Embargo. By a Member of the Irish
Parliament.
London. Cadell. Dublin Re-Printed. MDCCLXXX.
8vo. 30 pp.
H.C. 426.

360. Thoughts On News-Papers And A Free Trade.
Dublin : Hallhead. MDCCLXXX.
8vo. 31 pp.

361. A Letter To Travers Hartley, Esq; On The Subject Of The
Sugar Bill, And The Resolutions Of The Body Of Merchants.
Dublin : Byrne. MDCCLXXX.
8vo. 16 pp.
H.C. 426.

362. A Letter To The Earl Of Darnley, On The State Of The Poor
in Ireland.
London. Payne. MDCCLXXXI.
8vo. 21 pp. Signed W. Tighe.
H.C. 435.

363. Considerations Submitted To The People Of Ireland, On
Their Present Condition With Regard to Trade and Consti-
tution. In Answer To A Pamphlet, lately published, Entitled
" Observations on the Mutiny Bill, etc." ......
Dublin : Wilson. MDCCLXXXI.
8vo. 72 pp. b. t.
H.C. 432.

364. Rules, Orders, And Bye-Laws ; For The Good Government
Of The Corporation Of The Governor and Company Of The
Bank of Ireland.
n. d. n. p. (Probably 1782).
4to. 26 pp.
H.C. 438.

365. Outlines of a Plan for the Establishment of a National Bank
in the Kingdom of Ireland, etc.
In a Letter to
Dublin ?.
Reviewed in Hibernian Magazine, 1782, p. 288.
I have not been able to find this tract.

366. Junius Secundus's Letters To The People of Ireland, Against
The Establishment Of A National Bank.
Dublin : Marchbank. MDCCLXXXII.
8vo. 48 pp.

367. An Essay On The Necessity Of Protecting Duties.
>   *Dublin : Byrne.* MDCCLXXXIII.
>   8vo.   48 pp.   b. t.
>   *H.C.* 460.
>
>   Proposes a duty on foreign woollen goods imported into Ireland.

368. Considerations On The Effects Of Protecting Duties.
>   In A Letter To A Newly-Elected Member Of Parliament.
>   *Dublin : Wilson.* M,DCC,LXXXIII.
>   8vo.   45 pp.   b. t. and f. t.   Slip errata.
>   (By Robert Johnson).
>   *H.C.* 460.
>
>   In MS. on title "Published by the desire of Lord Shelburne, Secretary of State, R.J."
>   Very well written tract.

369. A Copy of The Charter Of The Corporation of the Governor and Company Of The Bank of Ireland.
>   *Dublin : W. Wilson.* M,DCC,LXXXIII.
>   Folio.   21 pp.
>   At the end there is "An Appendix, Containing A List of Governors, Directors, and Subscribers to the Bank of Ireland : With their several Subscription Sums affixed, in the Order they subscribed."
>
>   The "Gentleman's Magazine" of 1783 (p. 706), contains a short article describing the Arms and Seal of the Bank as the device of Georges Edmond Howard, who—the writer says—first proposed the Bank to the Government, and afterwards directed the plan on which it was founded.
>   A letter in the same Magazine of November 14, 1793, admits that it is questionable whether the advice was designed by Howard or not, but denies that he was the parent of the Bank.   On the contrary, it was moulded after the Bank of England, and the regulations and establishment of it were due to David La Touche and the Right Honourable John Foster, with the Assistance of a Mr. Hoffman, an ingenious merchant of Dublin, and Mr. Howard had even nothing to do with drawing up the Charter.
>   The Bank was chartered by the Act of 21-22 George III, Chapter XVI, and started business on the 1st of June, 1783, in St. Mary's Abbey.

LIST OF AUTHORS.